Endorsements

We will all walk the grief road at some time in our lives, which is why *Permission to Mourn* is such essential reading. Beautifully written, it is both sensitive and practical, yet not afraid to deal with the tough stuff. Ruth Potinu has produced a very different book from many others on the difficult subject of bereavement. Thankfully devoid of easy answers and thoughtless platitudes, she encourages us to exchange our preconceptions of how we, who are left behind, are 'supposed' to behave, and get on with the healing business of grieving. Between the covers of this book, information, wisdom, and reflective Scripture sit alongside the personal stories of people who have walked this painful road of suffering...and survived. And yet this is not a sad book. Rather, it is drenched with hope, and filled with an assurance that God is good...all the time, even through the darkest of journeys.

—Catherine Campbell, Author of *Broken Works Best* and *Journey with Me*

No one wants or expects to need a book on grief. But repeatedly I've found myself experiencing profound sorrow over the death of a loved one or close friend. As I tried to walk through those times of heart-wrenching loss, I've wanted something I could read or share, something that would offer understanding, comfort, and hope. Ruth Potinu has given us this in her book *Permission to Mourn*. Ruth has lived in several different cultures, and experienced deep loss, beginning with the death of her twin sister. She shares "grief stories" with an honesty that will resonate with those walking through hard times. It is comforting to know that you aren't alone. Thank you, Ruth, for writing a book that will give much-needed help and hope to many."

—Jamie Janosz, Managing Editor, *Today in the Word*, Author of *When Others Shuddered: Eight Women Who Refused to Give Up*

Permission to Mourn is the book you never want, but when you experience a deep loss are grateful exists. Rooted in the reality of loss and the sustaining grace of hearing from others who have walked a similar path, this book reminds you of the heart of our loving God who is deeply moved by your loss. *Permission to Mourn* is destined to become a must-read book.

—Amy Young, Author of *Looming Transitions* and founder of Global Trellis.

We all long for a community that gets us. And in different seasons of our lives, we find we need to lean on others who have gone before us, others who can be our guide. Ruth invites us to follow her as she guides us into her community of grief. She opens the door to a worldwide community of grievers and gives us permission to explore a better way to grieve. Scriptures and stories of others show us we aren't alone and provide an unexpected comfort to the mourning heart. This book is a gift. There are few communities we will all one day need to be welcomed into; grief is one of them. Ruth welcomes us here with hope and open arms.

—Denise Beck, Executive Director of Velvet Ashes

Grief is a part of everyone's life at one point or another. Ruth helpfully acknowledges that "grief is messy and uncomfortable without a lot of answers" while compiling stories of comfort and healing that point the reader to the God of all comfort who meets us in our grief. Anyone who finds themselves in a season of grieving or loss will find encouragement for their journey in these pages.

—Peter & Mary Frey daily vloggers of The Frey Life

Permission To Mourn

Engaging with Culture,
Story and Scripture
in a Quest for
Healing with Hope

RUTH POTINU

Permission to Mourn
Copyright © 2021 Ruth Potinu

All rights reserved. This book is protected by copyright laws of the United States of America. This book may not be copied or reprinted for commercial gain or profit.

Unless otherwise noted, scriptures are from The ESV® Bible (The Holy Bible, English Standard Version®), copyright © 2001 by Crossway, a publishing ministry of Good News Publishers. Used by permission. All rights reserved.

Scripture quotations marked (KJV) are from The Authorized (King James) Version. Rights in the Authorized Version in the United Kingdom are vested in the Crown. Reproduced by permission of the Crown's patentee, Cambridge University Press.

Scripture marked (NKJV) taken from the New King James Version®. Copyright © 1982 by Thomas Nelson. Used by permission. All rights reserved.

Scripture quotations marked (NIV) are taken from the Holy Bible, New International Version®, NIV®. Copyright © 1973, 1978, 1984, 2011 by Biblica, Inc.™ Used by permission of Zondervan. All rights reserved worldwide. www.zondervan.comThe "NIV" and "New International Version" are trademarks registered in the United States Patent and Trademark Office by Biblica, Inc.™

Scripture quotations marked (NLT) are taken from the Holy Bible, New Living Translation, copyright ©1996, 2004, 2015 by Tyndale House Foundation. Used by permission of Tyndale House Publishers, a Division of Tyndale House Ministries, Carol Stream, Illinois 60188. All rights reserved.

Cover Photo: Antonio Gaudi via Canva

This book is available at: www.milkandhoneybooks.com and other online retailers

Print ISBN 13: 978-1-953000-17-0
Ebook ISBN 13: 978-1-953000-18-7

For Worldwide Distribution

Dedication

These pages, these stories—this on-going grief journey; I have to dedicate to you, Allison Rebecca, my curly-haired, redheaded twin. 3,102 days on this earth does not feel like it was long enough at all, but I am grateful for each day that we did share together. You taught me so much during your beautiful, yet short, life.

You have taught me even more through your death.

*Blessed are those who mourn,
for they will be comforted.
—Matthew 5:4*

Table of Contents

INTRODUCTION   11

1 | IT'S OKAY NOT TO BE OKAY   15
    Mother's Day   19

2 | FREEDOM TO MOURN   27
    Plane Tickets, Doctor Pepper and Ever Present Grief   39

3 | CLEAN THE WOUND   47
    A Father's Love   56

4| THE CROWN DOES NOT PUT ON A SHOW   67
    Fading Photographs   75

5 | FINDING SOLACE IN STRUCTURE   83
    In the Process of Becoming   90

6 | WHEN LIFE IS GRIPPED BY FEAR   99
    The Strong One   110

7 | IS GOD GOOD TO ME?   119
    He Gives and Takes Away   132

8 | WASH YOUR FACE   143
    She Took Her First Breath in Heaven   151

9 | THE MINISTRY OF PAIN	**161**
I Know that Ache	170
10 | STOP! DON'T SAY THAT	**179**
I Love You Twice As Much	185
11 | IT'S COMPLICATED	**195**
Trigger Warning	202
12 | SURVIVING THE LANDMINES	**211**
The Sunshine of Life	219
13 | LEARNING TO LIVE AGAIN	**225**
A Child That Was Blessed	233
14 | SITTING WITH LAMENT, GRIEVING WITH HOPE	**239**
Lean Into the Pain	247
MEET THE CONTRIBUTORS	252
ABOUT THE AUTHOR	255
ACKNOWLEDGMENTS	256
ENDNOTES	260

Introduction

The day my eight-year-old twin sister suddenly left this world, the Congolese children's choir that she and I had been a part of sat outside our little brick home and just sang. "We don't often see white people die," a neighbor commented. "They always go back to their country when they are sick." Suddenly, our family had a ministry we never anticipated (and honestly never wanted)—the ministry of entering into grief and walking with those facing loss.

It is messy—so messy. It is painful, complicated, confusing, life altering and just plain hard. But, one thing that living in several different cultures has taught me is that grieving is a process, and this process is lightened within the context of community. Many cultures do grieve communally, and it does help ease the burden. But often in cultures that highly value self-help and the ability to say the right thing and fix problems, there is less space available for people to just sit with their grief and mourn the deep pain of loss. This can leave those who are facing a deep loss pulling in and pulling back during a time when they need to be reaching out to hold on to others and letting others (literally and figuratively) hold on to them.

What can be learned from cultures that create space for communal mourning? How can we, living in the midst of the busyness of modern life, bend to accommodate practices of grieving that have helped those in the past? What should we say to friends in the midst of grief, and what should we definitely avoid saying? My prayer is that through this book, this shared journey, we can begin to tackle some of these questions. Not that I have all the answers, but it is my hope that through personal stories (my own and others) and reflection on Biblical truths, we can move towards healthier ways to grieve. Let us start discussions about this often taboo topic, so that it no longer remains quite as taboo.

No one should have to grieve alone. Friend, my prayer as we journey through this difficult issue that everyone faces (or will likely face, at some point) is that you will feel less alone in your grief and that pieces of the stories shared on these pages will bring you hope and healing. May this book provide space for you to process, to grieve with hope and to learn how to better comfort the hurting who will inevitably cross your path. May these stories act as arms of a bigger community carrying you through and also opening doors for more in-person connection—because we need each other desperately.

As the body of Christ, let us commit to not shying away from painful topics like death and grief (even though they can leave us uncomfortable) and step into the battlefield in a sense—shoulder to shoulder—leaning on each other, weeping with each other and mourning together. We were not made for this broken world filled with death and disease, but we were created for a perfect home with the One who records all of our sorrows, the One who catches our tears in His bottle—the One who will one day wipe every tear from our eyes.

CHAPTER ONE

It's Okay Not To Be Okay

> *"Heaven knows we need never to be ashamed of our tears, for they are rain upon the blinding dust of earth, overlying our hard hearts. I was better after I cried than before."*
>
> —Charles Dickens (Pip in Great Expectations)

If you are reading this book and have lost someone close to you, I just want to say—I'm sorry. I'm sorry that it hurts so much and that you have experienced the kind of pain most people would not even wish on their worst enemy. I'm sorry that there are no easy answers or quick fixes. If I could, I would sit down on the floor next to you while you had a good cry—one of those messy cries that seems to help when there are just no words.

Do you know that tears can actually help jump-start the healing process? Biochemist Dr. William Frey (aka the tear expert) says that tears, produced as a response to emotions like sadness or pain, contain hormones that help the body deal with stress[1]. These "emotional" tears release endorphins into your body, which can actually help a person feel better. So, in a way, tears are a balm to ease pain. No wonder a good cry actually can help lift someone's mood.

In spite of the fact that tears were uniquely designed to help the human body deal with stress and pain, tears can often be seen as a sign of weakness. Modern culture especially likes to throw out sayings like, "Real men don't cry" or "Tears are for sissies". But, when Lazarus died, Jesus cried. He not only cried, John 11:35 says- "Jesus wept." This verse is one of the shortest verses in the Bible and yet such a potent one[2]. It shows just how deeply Christ empathized with people whose lives intertwined with His.

Jesus, the perfect Son of God, who flipped over tables and went toe to toe with the powerful religious leaders of the day, wept openly with his friends. He felt the deep grief that so many other people have felt ever since death first entered the world. He mourned in the face of death, weeping in community with Mary and Martha as they grieved their brother; and He grieved the friend He loved.

Losing a loved one hurts. No one would deny that. Yet many Christians, especially Christians raised with a more Western mindset, often have difficulty dealing openly with the pain of grief and can struggle to grieve in a healthy manner. I know I do. Even though I spent many formative years in Africa, my mindset is still very western and I often find myself conditioned to hold back tears instead of freely weeping with those who weep. It is a tough issue. I am much more comfortable grieving in private than in public; holding back the tears until I am alone and the lights are out.

It can also be tempting to think that it is somehow improper to grieve, especially for an extended period of time. So much emphasis seems to be put on holding it together and staying strong especially for those who have the hope of Christ. After all, we do have hope in life after death and in the resurrection. But while it is true that we have hope, it is also true that we are fragile humans and because we love—we will grieve. As long as we remain on this earth we *will* feel pain, and we need to express those feelings just as Jesus modeled so perfectly for us while He walked this earth.

1 Thessalonians 4:13-14 says, "Brothers and sisters, we do not want you to be uninformed about those who sleep in death, so that you do not grieve like the rest of mankind, who have no hope. For we believe that Jesus died and rose again, and so we believe that God will bring with Jesus those who have fallen asleep in him" (NIV). What a beautiful promise. There is hope in the resurrection. And yet, this verse is *not* telling us never to grieve, but rather *not* to grieve like those who have no hope in Christ.

Yes, there is hope! Often, we know that our loved ones are in heaven away from the pain and the sin of this broken world; and even when we do not have this hope to hold on to, we can trust in God's sovereignty. It is true that we should not grieve like those who have no hope, but we are *still* supposed to grieve. We just must grieve in a way that reflects the hope that anchors us.

In the Sermon on the Mount, Jesus told the crowd, "Blessed are those who mourn, for they shall be comforted" (Matthew 5:4). His words were not, "Stop sniffling. You are so short sighted. Toughen up, Buttercup." Instead, He promised comfort. One day Christ will establish His kingdom, and there will be no more death. "He will wipe every tear from their eyes, and there will be no more death or sorrow or crying or pain. All these things are gone forever"

(Revelation 21:4 NLT).

Until that time, here we are on earth; many days there will be tears. Grieving is a process, a long process, but that does not mean that life from now on will always be gloomy and teary. Yes, it will have its moments; but comfort comes and healing can happen. There is so much hope that we can cling to.

> "So you have sorrow now, but I will see you again; then you will rejoice, and no one can rob you of that joy."
> —John 16:22 (NLT)

Stories—the thing about stories is they have a way of pulling one in and pulling one through in a way that traditional prose can fall short. There is something comforting about hearing how someone continues to live, grow, survive, heal. So, tucked between each chapter of this book, is a personal essay written from a place of mourning. May these stories bring you comfort as your own story of healing is being written within you.

Mother's Day

By Amanda Prather

THE FINALITY OF death is something for which you can never be prepared. From an early age, we acquire the knowledge that when a person dies they aren't ever coming back. We learn about heaven and how they are in a better place, but no one can ever tell you what it's like to stare into a future without a loved one. The overwhelming feeling that comes over you as you try to wrap your mind around waking up every morning for the next ten, twenty, thirty years or more without that person is almost too much to bear. Often the body's natural defense system kicks in and the numbing feeling takes hold. I love the numbness. It is my protector—the one thing that makes each day without my mom bearable.

On Mother's Day 2011, I wrote my mom an email for her gift. She didn't have anything she wanted and enjoyed letters, so for her gift she asked me to write her a nice email. I sent her something that I hoped she would enjoy and that would make her feel loved and appreciated. I'd forgotten about the email until ten months later when I was sitting in the hospital room watching my mom lay in her bed like a vegetable, with only machines and modern medicine keeping her alive.

As my family and I spent the week in the hospital praying for her body and brain to recover, I began searching for anything that kept me close to her. I searched through my emails that we had shared and found the one I had sent her last Mother's Day. I told her how I loved and appreciated her and all the usual things, but I also told her that after her first battle with cancer, I hoped facing a life without her would be something that I would never have to experience. As I read that, I realized how real that fear had become.

I will never forget the morning I learned that my mom was sick. My sister and I shared an apartment, and she woke me to tell me that dad needed to talk to me. I took the phone, and he said that Mom was in the hospital. The way he said it, I presumed he was talking about his mom. He asked if I wanted to speak with her and I agreed. He handed the phone off and I heard my mom say hi. I think I felt my heart sink. It was that moment that I knew this wasn't good. We later learned that she had Stage IV leukemia.

For the next six years, she fought an off-and-on battle with the disease. I have seen things that I pray nobody ever has to experience. I watched my mom in so much pain. I saw her bald, fragile, scared, frustrated, angry and tired. The cancer aged her quickly. Her once strong and healthy body deteriorated quickly. Near the end, the pain was so bad that she couldn't walk on her own. She shuffled around the house with a walker. When I would come home to visit, I would sometimes hear the walker at night going across our hardwood floor. It was such a creepy sound, and I would tease her about how it sounded like a killer from a horror movie coming for you. I had to help my mom use the bathroom.

Nothing broke my heart more than that. She didn't even have the strength to get up and off the toilet like a normal person.

The cancer was very aggressive at the end. The doctors wanted her to get a second bone marrow transplant. I think we all knew it wasn't good and the chance of death was very possible, even if we didn't want to admit it. After the first bone marrow transplant, my dad took a leave of absence from work to take care of her, and this time they asked me to do so. On my last day of work before my leave, I got a call from my dad saying my mom had a serious lung infection. There is a feeling of dread that hits, and I just couldn't shake it. I knew. And I hated that feeling.

I headed up there a couple days later so my dad could return to work. The doctors told me she was doing much better than she had been doing, but nothing prepared me for that day. I walked into her room and saw the shell of the woman who raised me. Bald and fragile, her eyes were almost completely yellow. She had completed the bone marrow transplant, and it had caused raw open wounds all in her mouth and throat. Her eyes were sunken, and she looked like her mom had at eighty years old. The transplant had created a blockage in her intestine, and the doctors wouldn't let her eat or drink anything for fear of it bursting. The infection was causing confusion, and at times she didn't know where she was. The worst part was a moment when she didn't even know me. The nurses allowed me to feed her tiny ice chips when she felt up to it. The pain in her mouth was so bad that she could barely open it for me to put them in. The ice relieved her thirst but burned her mouth at the same time. The open wounds caused large amounts of mucus in her mouth that they had to suction causing her even more pain.

In her entire battle with cancer, including the moment of her death, those two days of watching her in so much pain were by far the most difficult moments. At the end of the second night, my mom's heart stopped. They revived her, but she spent the next week in a vegetative state her life slowly slipping away. And then, after a week, I watched the woman who raised me, loved me completely, supported me, and was my best friend pass away in front of her two daughters and husband.

The pain is still very much there although you slowly learn how to cope. I always heard people say how life goes on after a loss, but it's weird to actually experience the impact of that. In the grieving process, the instinct is to hold on. You want to grab hold of anything and everything that makes you feel as if that person is still alive. The knowledge of their death is there, but the reality hasn't hit the heart and you want everything to remain still. But, life doesn't work that way. It does go on. It feels like being in a mob of people who are almost pushing you forward in spite of your firm stance to stay in one spot. But the movement has to happen. It is the world's way of doing its best to make you cope.

The process of coping isn't easy. Some days it's tolerable, some days it's numbing and other days it's torture. Loss is huge and final. That's why the numbness can feel like a best friend. The days when it seems too much, my body comes to my defense and the emotional anesthetic kicks in. I find that the numbness is usually pretty strong, but it's the odd things that break through that barrier and pierce my heart into reality. When my mom was sick, the American Cancer Society graciously gave hospital seminars that helped patients do their best to feel and look good. I was going through her goodie bag and found a makeup sponge that she had used. I held it knowing that this object had once touched her face. It was enough to make me burst into tears. Then there was the day I found the clothes we bought for her that past Christmas. She had loved them but never got the chance to wear them—crying ensued once again. Moments that happen at random and often show up so unexpectedly. I could be having the best day and on the way home from work, my mind switches and tears flow down my face. Or the times when I am tired, stressed or just need advice; I don't know where to go anymore because the person I went to, to help me through all of those things, is now gone. I have often never felt more lost.

But, I suppose that with every hardship in life, there are lessons to be learned. I saw my mom let fear dictate a lot of her choices. She waited until the end of her life to start doing things she had always wanted to do but was too afraid to attempt. Through her death, she has helped me move forward in the ways that I had been afraid to go. I have also learned that I can survive much more than I ever thought I could. About a month and half after my mom passed, her sister had a stroke and died just a few days later. I was distraught, to say the least, and struggled with reliving my mom's death as well as coping with my aunt's. I craved intimacy in a way that I never had, physical and emotional. I couldn't sleep for more than two hours. I had thoughts and anxiety of more people I loved dying. I wanted to cover my pain with alcohol. I didn't know what to do.

By the grace of God, a wonderful lady, I had known for many years and who is a professional counselor, called to ask if she could act as a weekly life coach for me as part of a homework assignment for a certificate she was in the process of earning. I learned through this counseling that I can make it. I have learned that I need to talk to people to help me, and I have learned what it means to go through hell and come back even stronger.

There are so many emotions and feelings that accompany the death of someone close to you. It's hard to verbalize the pain, but try. That's the process of grief-trying. Some days you may want to talk to others, some you want to be alone, some days are filled with tears and some days you just need to go out and laugh and forget all the pain in your heart. You may confuse people or hurt them or feel misunderstood and alone. But, you wake up the next morning and you try to go forward again. You never get it down perfectly. You just do what you can to make it. There is life beyond our loss and as hard as it is, you will survive. You may kick and fight through it, but you will make it.

A Psalm for Reflection

Forsake Me Not When My Strength Is Spent

Psalm 71

In you, O LORD, do I take refuge;
let me never be put to shame!
In your righteousness deliver me and rescue me;
incline your ear to me, and save me!
Be to me a rock of refuge,
to which I may continually come;
you have given the command to save me,
for you are my rock and my fortress.
Rescue me, O my God, from the hand of the wicked,
from the grasp of the unjust and cruel man.
For you, O Lord, are my hope,
my trust, O LORD, from my youth.
Upon you I have leaned from before my birth;
you are he who took me from my mother's womb.
My praise is continually of you.
I have been as a portent to many,
but you are my strong refuge.
My mouth is filled with your praise,
and with your glory all the day.
Do not cast me off in the time of old age;
forsake me not when my strength is spent.
For my enemies speak concerning me;
those who watch for my life consult together
and say, "God has forsaken him;
pursue and seize him,

for there is none to deliver him."
O God, be not far from me;
O my God, make haste to help me!
May my accusers be put to shame and consumed;
with scorn and disgrace may they be covered
who seek my hurt.
But I will hope continually
and will praise you yet more and more.
My mouth will tell of your righteous acts,
of your deeds of salvation all the day,
for their number is past my knowledge.
With the mighty deeds of the Lord God I will come;
I will remind them of your righteousness, yours alone.
O God, from my youth you have taught me,
and I still proclaim your wondrous deeds.
So even to old age and gray hairs,
O God, do not forsake me,
until I proclaim your might to another generation,
your power to all those to come.
Your righteousness, O God,
reaches the high heavens.
You who have done great things,
O God, who is like you?
You who have made me see many troubles and calamities
will revive me again;
from the depths of the earth
you will bring me up again.
You will increase my greatness
and comfort me again.
I will also praise you with the harp
for your faithfulness, O my God;
I will sing praises to you with the lyre,
O Holy One of Israel.

CHAPTER TWO

Freedom to Mourn

> *"How long has it been for you? It's been 20 for me. They say the first year is the hardest, but they're all hard if you ask me."*
>
> — Angela Lansburry (Mrs. 'Arris Goes to Paris)

As I type this, my aunt (my dad's only sibling) is on life support and my best friend's grandpa is at home under hospice care. I am thousands of miles away, and it is a hard time to be away. Grief is a heavy reality. It does not matter if your loved one was nine weeks old, still in utero, or ninety-nine years old with a full life behind them—each unique person fills a space that no one else can ever fill. When a person's physical presence is no longer present on this blue ball, the space that they leave behind can never be filled by anyone else; and so we grieve.

The question becomes where will that grief take you? Grief is a sign of love. It is rare to truly grieve someone or something that you did not actually cherish on some level. Many times, grief can actually pull someone into a closer relationship with God. For others, deep loss can also bring with it a loss of faith because the pain feels too much. "How could God let this happen?" "Can I continue to trust a God who allowed this to happen?"

Grief is a journey, and that journey will look different for everyone. The important thing is not so much *how* you process and work through your grief but that you take the time to do so. Stuffing feelings of grief into a dark emotional closet and hoping that they go away is not healing (*more on that in chapter 3*). One way to heal is to actively process, actively seek comfort and actively move towards a new normal. The fact that this book is in your hands is a great start. It is best not to walk the journey of grief alone, and if the words in this book help you take steps forward and give you space and time to mourn in a healthy manner, then its purpose is fulfilled.

In her book, *It's Ok That You're Not Ok: Meeting Grief and Loss in a Culture that Doesn't Understand,* psychotherapist Megan Devine shares how her perspective on grief was flipped on its head after her partner drowned. She points out that we live in a culture that is obsessed with fixing things and happy endings but grief cannot be "fixed". Grief can only be experienced. "Our culture sees grief as a kind of malady: a terrifying, messy emotion that needs to be cleaned up and put behind us as soon as possible. As a result we have outdated beliefs around how long grief should last and what it should look like. We see it as something to fix, rather than something to tend to or support. Even our clinicians are trained to see grief as a disorder rather than a natural response to deep loss."[3]

As someone who comes from the field of counseling and sees some of the flaws with the current system, what does Devine see as a solution to outdated models of trying to "fix" grief? "The real cutting edge of growth and development," she says, "Is in hurting with each other. It's in companionship, not correction. Acknowledgement—being seen and heard and witnessed inside the truth about one's own life—is the only real medicine of grief."[4] As a culture, it is time to stop trying to look for that silver lining to somehow make grief better or force a "happy ever after" fairytale ending when there just isn't one. It is time to admit that grief hurts deeply. This world is broken and things can't always be made right again.

Just this week, a mom in a group that I am a part of, was lamenting the fact that she recently had a miscarriage and now, several months later, she and her family were in the middle of a big move. As the family is in the process of packing, multiple people have said to her, "Well at least you're not pregnant while trying to move." As if somehow it was a good thing that her baby died. How insensitive! Yet well-meaning people say these types of things all the time to those in the midst of grief because our culture is overly desperate to find good in painful situations. Maybe instead of trying to finish everyone's story with, "And they moved on, and lived happily ever after"; we should be content with "And they learned how to carry their pain as they continued to journey

> Maybe instead of trying to finish everyone's story with, "And they moved on, and lived happily ever after": we should be content with "And they learned how to carry their pain as they continued to journey through life."

through life." Death in itself is not good, even though God can bring about good from even the most painful moments possible. Death is from the enemy, and one day it will be conquered for all of eternity.

Scripture is full of stories, real raw stories, which often show individuals in the midst of grief. The psalmist David was no stranger to pain, and grief touched his life over and over. His newborn baby, born to Bathsheba, died. His daughter Tamar was raped by her half-brother Amnon. Amnon was then murdered at the command of his half-brother Absalom. Absalom met a violent death in battle when he tried to replace David as Israel's king. It is no wonder that the Psalms David wrote are frequently grief soaked prayers filled with raw lament. And yet, in the midst of a life so tainted by grief—again and again the Psalms record David pouring his grief out to God and then ultimately finding comfort and joy in his Lord. Psalm 43 recounts one of David's many struggles as he mourned while being pursued by his enemies.

> *Why must I go about mourning,*
> *oppressed by the enemy?*
> *Send me your light and your faithful care,*
> *Let them lead me;*
> *let them bring me to your holy mountain,*
> *to the place where you dwell.*
> *Then I will go to the altar of God,*
> *to God, my joy and my delight.*
> —Psalms 43:2-3 (NIV)

It is interesting to note that in the process of mourning David was not afraid to openly share his struggles with God. He did not pretend that life was easy or all sunshine and rainbows when it was pulling him down to the depths. He did not shy away from communicating with his Creator when life was not as pain-free as he may have liked. He let his struggles take him to the source of comfort. He clearly expressed that he did not want to stay in the state of mourning that he found himself in. David turned to God and asked Him for two things: *light and faithful care.* In the midst of grief, care is needed. Individuals in mourning are often unable to care for themselves well. Light brings hope, illuminating a way out of the darkness that threatens to swallow one whole.

Light and care brought David from a place of oppression and led him to God's holy mountain—the place where he found God to dwell. David's journey led him to God's altar and at that altar David says he found not only joy but also delight.

God is not distant in times of grief. He is ever ready to provide comfort, but too often comfort is sought apart from God and these comforts, like excessive alcohol, binge watching TV shows and even certain medications, only numb—they do not heal the pain. Please hear me carefully on this one, medication *can* have a very real part to play in both physical and emotional healing; but if a medication is only numbing pain while the source is left bleeding out, how can long term healing truly happen?

While on this earth, there will always be pain at some level. This is just part of the reality of living in a world marred by sin. But that does not mean that one has to stay forever in a place of deep pain. Our loved ones, who are no longer on this earth, would not want us to remain forever in a place of constant pain. It is not in God's loving heart to leave His children in the shadow of the valley of death forever. We may walk through many valleys of death, but as our good shepherd, Christ promises to lead us out of the valley. These valleys of death are not meant to be camped in, but walked through. And after the valleys, we must seek God in the mountains; just as David did in Psalm 43 for there—in the presence of God—promised joy and delight are found.

Not everyone's journey of mourning will be the same. Some people process loss by talking it out, others by spending time in nature, some find journaling to be healing and others process through music. Some people, like my dad, need a physical project; which is why when my twin sister died he found it healing to build her coffin—a final act of love. Many times a professional counselor can help as a guide on the path to healing. The important thing is to take time and discover what works for you. How has God uniquely wired you and what do you find helps heal your soul?

Having lived in several cultures, I have noticed that in today's fast-paced world many cultures do not naturally give much space for expressing grief in a corporate manner. We have spaces for corporate worship, corporate giving, learning and teaching, but apart from an often brief time of visitation and the funeral service—grief is left to be processed in private. This can leave people feeling very alone and even desperate during a time when the comforting arms of community are needed most.

It is not only that there is not a natural space for mourning as a community, but people in more fast-paced modern cultures often find that the community they did have before the loss of a loved one can actually shrink dramatically because people just do not know how to act towards a friend who is facing loss. Sometimes even good friends will end up avoiding the person who is hurting causing even *more* emotional pain and an even deeper sense of loss. A mom in the community where I went to high school had a son who was killed in a car accident. She expressed that she felt an extra layer of hurt saying that after her son's death the people who used to chat with her in the grocery store started avoiding her after the accident because they did not know what to say. This understandably left her feeling very alone and abandoned by the people she desperately longed for comfort from.

I, too, noticed this acutely after my friend Alice's sudden death. My friend Alice was a doctoral student from Kenya who was just months away from graduating with her PhD when a brain aneurysm suddenly took her life. I say friend, but she was more of an adopted family member who was frequently at our house and brought so much light and sweet laughter wherever she went. I will always treasure the many, many, many cups of chai (tea) we consumed together discussing everything from Jane Austin to how to properly roll a chapati.

After her passing, I found myself surrounded by many of her colleagues, friends and fellow students, most from various parts of Africa, as we gathered to plan her memorial service. The memory of that afternoon is blurred in part due to the acute pain that we were all feeling; but I remember a sense of openness, sharing food, stories, songs and even some laughter with people, the majority of whom I had just met that afternoon. We found mutual comfort in just talking openly about how much Alice meant to us and remembering the incredible woman she was.

Mid-week I went to church to help out with a children's program. It was the church that Alice would often attend when she spent weekends with my family. By that point, most people had heard the news of Alice's passing; yet as I interacted with people that evening only one person briefly brought up what had just happened. Many of us, from that church, were grieving; but we were grieving silently not wanting or knowing how to openly approach the grief we were experiencing. All of us, most likely, were waiting and hoping that someone else would say something first, but no one seemed sure how to start.

It can be uncomfortable but healthy to learn how to mourn in community openly acknowledging the pain of loss. Not that grief must always be processed in a public setting. When Jesus received news that his cousin, John the Baptist, had been beheaded, Matthew 14:13 says, "he withdrew from there in a boat to a desolate place by himself." But, while there is comfort in grieving in private, it is also healing to be willing to share feelings of grief openly.

This month marks a year since my husband's aunt passed away and just about every time we drive past the street where her house is, a part of me still misses her deeply. Her house is still there. Relatives continue to live there, but without her presence it is just not the same. I remember the times I spent at her house when we first arrived in Papua New Guinea. We had very broken conversations as I slowly learned to speak Tok Pisin. I remember sitting with her as we mourned the death of her husband just a week before my son was born. I think about how, a year later, she bought our son's first birthday cake. It was a huge cake so big that there was enough for all the village kids to have a slice. I remember hugging her goodbye at the airport as she flew to the Philippians for cancer treatment that we all hoped would add some more years to her life. That farewell at the airport was the last time I saw her responsive. After months of treatment, she used her last energy reserves to fly home. As she lay on a thin mattress out on her wooden veranda with an IV hanging from a wooden beam and her sister faithfully rubbing her swollen legs, it was clear that she would not be with us much longer. I longed to tell her that we were expecting a little girl, but by that point her frail body and mind were past being able to process new information.

This past Sunday, at church, her best friend held my daughter, Allyson. Often when she sees baby Allyson she holds her close to her chest, with her check touching my daughter's check. She rocks her and often as she rocks her she softly cries a melodic, rhythmic cry. Tears will stream down her cheeks for a few minutes as she thinks of her friend and how she would have loved to have met little Allyson. Then she will smile, and with eyes still moist, hand Allyson back to me.

Mourning is a very visible part of PNG culture. When someone dies the little world surrounding that person stops. A week-long haus krai (house cry) will start which typically involves creating a space (usually outside) for people to come and literally just sit and cry with the family. A tarp is often spread on the ground and a temporary shelter erected to provide some shade and protection from rain and sun. If the death takes place in the city, the haus krai typically happens in the evening. When people get off work, they usually come bringing scones (bread rolls) and money to help the family cover funeral expenses as it is rare for someone here to have insurance as a means to cover funeral costs. Your village is your insurance in a way. In the village, haus krais are often an all day affair. Gardening stops, work stops, relatives and friends from surrounding villages come. People sit together late into the night often sharing a simple meal of tea and kaukau (sweet potatoes). No one is left alone during that initial time of grief.

As someone coming from a more western/individualistic culture, I often struggle with how publicly grief is expressed here. It is beautiful and so healing, but so far from what I am used to that it can often be uncomfortable. I find myself standing awkwardly when the friend of my husband's aunt holds Allyson and openly sheds tears as she remembers her best friend. I often feel that I need to say or do something, but I have no words. Which (thankfully) is okay here—no words are expected. I am learning that this is often what grief truly is—messy and uncomfortable without a lot of answers.

Sitting on the ground at a haus krai can feel strange. Again, I do not have any magic words to suddenly fix things, but no words are required, just a person's presence and their tears. What can you say really? In more Western cultures people will often say to someone grieving, "Let me know if you need anything? Or "Let me know what I can do?" But, frequently someone in the midst of grief cannot really process what he or she needs. Maybe they need a hot meal, or someone to take care of their laundry for a week, or they might love for someone to watch their kids at the park for an afternoon. Try to step in someone's shoes for a bit and think practically because often those facing loss are too physically and emotionally drained to come up with ideas of how someone can help, but that does not mean that practical help is not greatly appreciated.

A way to phrase the question in a more practical way would be to do as much thinking for the person as possible so that they can answer with a simple yes or no question like "Would it be helpful for you if I brought over some dinner tonight?" or "Would you like me to ride along with you when you go to the funeral home to make arrangements?" Allow a person to accept help or pass on it depending on if what you are offering is something they would find comforting. The person is then free from having to do the mental work of trying to think of specific ideas during a time when one is often too exhausted to think clearly.

I'm learning that sometimes the best thing you can do for someone in the midst of grief is to just be there. Go out for coffee, wrap them in a hug and let them stay there for as long as they need to. Don't ask them if they are ok. (They aren't ok. How could they be?) Don't feel the need to ask them how they are doing. (It's most likely they are not doing well at that moment. How could they be?) Let them cry. Be there. Be silent. Give them space to process, feel, cry some ugly tears or maybe not shed any tears at all. Listen to stories of the person they loved. Send a text to tell them you are thinking about them. Talk about things—even more normal things. Go for a walk together, and when they are ready, talk about the hard things, the raw pain, the disturbing thoughts, whatever they feel that they need to process. Be that safe space. Resist the temptation to run away from the awkwardness, and commit to embracing the messy mourning process.

Since starting this chapter my best friend's grandfather passed away. The funeral was this weekend. My sister also sent me a message to say my aunt, who has been in a drug-induced coma, is no longer responsive. A very big part of me wants to hop on a plane right now just so that I can give my grandma a hug. Many times the circumstances that you find yourself in, when grief hits, are far from ideal. Many times numbness is the only feeling that comes. Sometimes you want the whole world to stop and the sun not to come up. How can people continue to go to work and go about their day when your world has shattered?

I think that is part of the reason that huas kais can be such a comfort here in PNG. The community does pause out of respect for the family and respect for the person who has passed on. A public holiday was just declared for tomorrow for a head of state who recently passed away to give time and space, for those who want to, to show their respect and attend the funeral. Wouldn't it be nice if more countries did this—a pause, time to process, to pay respect to those who are no longer here? It makes me think of the Israelites taking 30 days to mourn the death of their leader Moses. There is so much to learn from these types of practices. As much as possible, give yourself those initial 30 days to really sit with loss before feeling too pressured to get back to life as it was. It is so tempting to "deal" with the pain of grief by staying busy. But, a deep wound that is ignored or simply covered up will not properly heal. We need to give ourselves space to heal and freedom to mourn what has been lost.

"Weeping may last through the night,
but joy comes with the morning."
—Psalm 30:5b (NLT)

Plane Tickets, Doctor Pepper and Ever Present Grief

By Amy Post

NO PERSON EVER has a desire to experience grief. It is a pain that lasts the rest of your life and can't be treated with anything but time. But, grief is evidence of deep love. It's the price for love, even. However, that doesn't mean it will all look the same for everyone. Grief looks different for every person, because every person is different, every relationship is different and every loss is different. So why would we expect our grief to look the same?

My world shifted with a phone call. I was sitting at home watching TV when my mom called me and told me that my younger brother, David, who was 20 at the time, had been swept away in a river in Arkansas. He'd been swimming with friends, and the current was too strong for him. At first, I just thought of the inconvenience. He was carried down the river and would have to walk back. My mind was already trying to protect me from the fear and grief. That's when the waiting started. The thought crossed my mind that he could be gone, but I dismissed it just as quickly. I followed Facebook posts of people who lived near him and were involved in the search...more waiting. As darkness settled, I became more and more fearful, but I was just too far away. I wanted to fly to Arkansas, but if I did that, it would be admitting that something was really wrong. So, I kept waiting.

My best friend drove an hour and a half to wait with me. There was amazing relief in not being alone. Every hour that passed that night made it more and more clear to me that this was far more than an inconvenience. The fear just kept building and building. Eventually, all I could do was pray "Jesus, Jesus" over and over. The night passed and there was still no word. I called in to work the next day and just kept waiting. Finally, my best friend told me that she had bought me an airline ticket to Arkansas. She said, at this point, regardless of the outcome, I needed to be with my family. She was right.

I flew to Arkansas the next day. My boyfriend at the time, (husband now) Marcus, offered to come with me. I still regret not taking him up on his offer. I remember calling him to tell him David was missing and thinking, "This is it. Today I find out if this is the man I'm going to marry." I thank God that our relationship was at the point that he could be what I needed over the next days and weeks.

I made it to Arkansas and continued waiting. What followed was three more days of searching the river, bloodhounds, cadaver dogs, fear, laughter and camaraderie, exhaustion, and a growing understanding that my brother would not be coming home. Finally, four days after he went swimming, his earthly body was found, not far from where he jumped into the water.

Grief. Profound grief. Yet, at the same time, my emotions shut off. They gathered our family and a local pastor came to tell us that his body had been found. I didn't cry. I couldn't. I had to be strong for my other siblings. I saw the hearse drive past and just felt disconnected. The grief, while ever present, took a back burner to planning a funeral in Arkansas and a memorial service in Wisconsin. I broke down just a little, while I was talking with my sister. She immediately started sobbing. I knew my grief had to stay locked up until it was 'safe'.

We had a beautiful funeral and memorial. Many many people loved my brother and were impacted by his life. David was full of life. Everything he did, he went after with enthusiasm and excitement. If you needed help moving, he'd show up laughing and ready to help. He encouraged everyone he knew at every opportunity. He served whether he was asked or not. He gave the BEST hugs and somehow knew just when they were needed. I spent many of the last years of his life living in Seattle, Washington while he lived in Wisconsin; so we talked on the phone to keep in touch. Every time we spoke, he would tell me about some person he cared about who he wanted me to pray for. He left gaping holes everywhere he was known.

All through both the funeral and memorial I still didn't cry. Too many people needed to be comforted by me. Strange, isn't it? Most people who I spoke with that day wanted to talk about David, but they weren't doing it to comfort me, but to be comforted. I could see the difference when someone spoke to me who truly understood loss. Typically it was just a hug, or a whispered "I'm so sorry." When those people spoke with me, my emotions rose to the surface and I struggled again to keep them in check. What didn't help was "Are you ok?" or "How are you feeling?" The asker didn't actually want the answers to those questions. If I answered honestly, they might never actually speak to me again.

It was almost two weeks before I made it back home to Seattle.

Once I was home, I was dealing with the loss all day, every day. I was dealing with my grief basically on my own now. Marcus, (my husband now) listened to me and supported me in profound ways. He said and did all the right things, and he still supports me in my journey of grief to this day. But, it wasn't his loss. All of the people who I shared my loss with were half a country away. I had to go to work. I had to interact with other humans who hadn't just suffered a significant loss. The hardest part at that point was all of the insensitive things people said, trying to help. I had one person compare losing my brother to losing their dog. Others offered empty platitudes like "heaven just needed another angel" or "his work on earth was done." Someone else even went so far as to say "He's probably better off leaving this awful world anyway." I learned quickly that people who haven't suffered loss don't really understand what to say to someone going through it. They had truly kind intentions, but fell so short of actually helping. I started to translate all of the awful things people said into "I love you. I'm here for you."

The best analogy for grief I have ever heard compares the loss of a loved one with losing a limb. The actual wound hurts a lot at first, but it heals. The harder part is living without that limb. Every facet of life has to be re-learned to accommodate for the missing part. I didn't really cry until about a month and a half after David died. My brother Jon got married, and I just lost it in the middle of the ceremony. It was the first major moment where I felt the hole that my brother had left behind.

Grief wears so many faces—sometimes it's deep sadness, sometimes it's exhaustion or depression. Other times it's anger or guilt. It's been almost ten years since my brother died. Now, for me, grief is usually a small shadow to every happy moment. I miss what should have been. I sobbed the day before my wedding because all I wanted in the world was for him to be there. He never met my husband. I thought of David and wept the day each of my daughters was born. David would have been a wonderful uncle. He has five nieces and nephews now and would be loving on them and spoiling them rotten. Every holiday, every family visit, the Chicago Cubs winning the World Series... All of these came with their side of grief.

Eventually, grief can even show itself as laughter. David loved Dr. Pepper. I mean LOVED it. Not too long ago, I came out of Target and there was an empty Dr. Pepper can sitting on top of my van. I laughed out loud and was able to carry that through the rest of my day.

Ravi Zacharias said, "Time is not a healer, it is only a revealer of how God does the healing." This is so true. My grief looks different today than it did the day we lost David. But, my God looks different to me today than He did the day David died. The day I lost my brother was the day I knew, deep within my soul, that I needed my Heavenly Father. He alone could sustain me through this loss. Before that day, I had a relationship with Christ. I had lived my life for Him for a long time. But, that day, I learned real, true dependence on Christ. I also learned that God could handle my grief, my anger and my questioning. The loss of my brother began a season of transparency with my Heavenly Father that I had never experienced before. If I am being truly honest, I would admit that I'd undo all of the good to have him back. But, I'm so thankful that through all of it, my Heavenly

Father has been present and attentive. He has truly given "a crown of beauty instead of ashes, the oil of joy instead of mourning, and a garment of praise instead of a spirit of despair" (Isaiah 61:3 NIV).

A Psalm for Reflection

Psalm 43

Vindicate me, my God,
and plead my cause
against an unfaithful nation.
Rescue me from those who are
deceitful and wicked.
You are God my stronghold.
Why have you rejected me?
Why must I go about mourning,
oppressed by the enemy?
Send me your light and your faithful care,
let them lead me;
let them bring me to your holy mountain,
to the place where you dwell.
Then I will go to the altar of God,
to God, my joy and my delight.
I will praise you with the lyre,
O God, my God.
Why, my soul, are you downcast?
Why so disturbed within me?
Put your hope in God,
for I will yet praise him,
my Savior and my God (NIV).

CHAPTER THREE

Clean the Wound

"It has been said, 'time heals all wounds.' I do not agree. The wounds remain. In time, the mind, protecting its sanity, covers them with scar tissue and the pain lessens. But it is never gone."

—Rose Fitzgerald Kennedy

I became an unwilling front row student to the importance of properly cleaning a wound last year. I was rushing around one day (as moms of two young kids tend to rush around), and as I came out of the bathroom I pulled the door shut behind me and cut my ankle on a metal piece that my husband had screwed to the bottom of the door. Life in the tropics can often be hard on poorly made wooden doors, and the bottom half of the door was starting to slowly disintegrate.

I felt the sharp pain of the cut, and I knew it was a deep one. I was juggling a baby who seemed to want to nurse constantly and a bunch of other things that at the time felt really important, so I did not even take time to clean the cut properly. We were out of Band-Aids, so I didn't even cover it. I planned to take care of it—later. I planned to pick up some Band-Aids the next time I was at the store, but I just never got around to it.

Even though the cut was deep, at first it didn't give me too much trouble. It seemed to be healing. I did not really give it much thought, to be honest. But then that uncovered wound got infected. Suddenly a wound that I thought was healing was an angry red, and I could barely put any weight on it.

I could have gone to the clinic the first day the cut started to flare up, but I did not. There was a playgroup that I had been looking forward to, so we went to that instead. I was also mourning the fact that my amazing friends, who used to run the clinic we went to as a family, had recently moved. In the back of my mind, I guess I knew that popping into the clinic just would not be the same as it used to be. So, instead of going to the clinic (which has some excellent, well-trained nurses) I dressed the infected wound myself, lamented the fact that my medical friends were no longer a phone call away and hobbled miserably through the entire playgroup trying to act like it was no big deal when in reality I was in severe pain.

The next day my husband was preaching at a funeral. Then it was the weekend and the clinic was closed. At the recommendation of a friend, I went to a medical friend of hers who worked out of a back room of her house (PNG life can be a bit sketchy at times) and got a shot of something (probably some type of antibiotic). But, that random doctor/nurse (I'm not even sure) did not even look at the wound. The shot brought some temporary relief, but the wound was far from healed.

That next week we had an overseas team coming for a visit, so instead of going to the clinic (like a sane person!) I hopped around on one foot cleaning the entire house. Bad choice, I know. That cut turned into a deep, deep wound that kept getting worse until I finally went to the proper clinic (where I should have gone to in the first place) and gave it the attention it deserved. Because I neglected to treat the cut when it was much smaller, it took four long months to fully heal. I still have a scar on the back of my ankle from that cut, and that scar will stay with me the rest of my life. It serves as a visual reminder that wounds need to be properly cleaned and treated. It does not matter if you think you are too busy or just would rather do other things than seek treatment—if you do not take care of a wound it will fester until the pain is so bad that you cannot ignore it anymore. An untreated wound can even get to the point where it could cost a person their life.

Emotional wounds also need healing. They will fester if ignored. They will start to throb and might even smell in a way (through harmful words or actions towards yourself or towards others) just like an untreated physical wound can start to smell.

My husband and I work with widows and their children here in PNG, and one book we use in part to help the ladies process some of the emotional pain that they have lived through is called *Healing the Wounds of Trauma*. This book includes a helpful chart that compares and contrasts physical wounds and heart (or emotional) wounds.[5]

Emotional wounds may not be as visible as physical wounds; but, just like with physical wounds, neglecting to treat them will only result in more pain down the road.

PHYSICAL WOUND	HEART WOUND
It is visible	It is invisible, but shows up in the person's behavior.
It is painful, and must be treated with care.	It is painful, and must be treated with care.
If ignored, it is likely to get worse.	If ignored, it is likely to get worse.
It must be cleaned to remove any foreign objects or dirt.	The pain has to come out, and any sin must be confessed.
If the wound heals on the surface with infection still inside, it will cause the person to become very sick.	If people pretend their emotional wounds are healed when really they are not, it will cause the person greater problems.
Only God can bring healing, but he often uses people and medicine to do so.	Only God can bring healing but he often uses people and an understanding of how our emotions heal to do so.
If not treated, it attracts flies.	If not treated, it attracts sin.
It takes time to heal.	It takes time to heal.
A healed wound leaves a scar.	A healed heart wound also leaves a scar. People can be healed, but they will not be exactly the same as they were before the wound.

One way physical wounds can be treated is by cleaning them with a sterile solution such as saline. Emotional wounds are often healed through processing the pain. It takes time. It can feel messy.

It can hurt, but healing—slow healing from the inside out—can happen, and must happen, for the sake of a person's overall health. Emotional wounds can be cleaned in different ways. Counseling is one way to process and cleanse. Maybe emotional cleaning will come from sitting with a friend or family member and honestly talking through what is going on in your head. Processing can happen through journaling, writing a letter, or just taking some time out to sit in nature and have a good cry. Maybe healing for you will begin through song or prayer. David does this often in the Psalms getting all his emotions out, even the ugly ones—taking them to the source—to God who can handle those emotions. God is the one who placed emotions in us, so there is no need to pretend that things are ok when they are not. Be real in your prayers. God already can see to the core of your heart, and He is not put off by the intensity of emotion. If there was ever a safe place to express emotion, it is with the one who created emotions.

Deep wounds (even those of the heart) need to be covered and protected from harsh elements. Not everyone you meet will be able to help you heal from emotional wounds. At times, it can be easy to over share with those who are not in a place to help provide wise counsel or a needed listening ear. If an emotional wound is receiving harsh or uncaring words, those words can sting as opposed to being a healing balm. Use discretion with whom you allow to look at your emotional wounds of grief. Maybe it will be a professional counselor, or a friend who knows you well; maybe it will be a family member or someone who has walked through a similar type of grief. When processing through pain with someone, start small; see how they respond and then, if there is peace, begin to delve into the deeper wounds.

    Just like with physical wounds, emotional wounds often take time to heal, especially the deep ones. Here in PNG people who have lost an immediate family member will often wear a simple red strip of cloth tied around their wrist for the first year after their loved one's passing. I love this because it serves as a quiet sign of the healing process. Yes, the person is still functioning and going about their year, but you can see a visible sign, even on a stranger, that they recently lost someone close to them. That simple strip of red cloth is also comforting, in a sad way, by how common it is—a reminder that you are not the only person who is processing loss. You see neighbors, church members, the man in front of you in the line at the bank, all wearing that strip of red cloth. It is like a silent nod—I'm there too, grieving in a parallel space—and it makes one realize that grief is not as lonely as it can often feel.

    One way of healing from grief is to allow yourself time to process- not pushing difficult feelings down but letting them out and letting the healing process begin. There is a tendency, especially in Christian circles, to just want a quick prayer or maybe even a miracle to take place so that, boom, healing has happened now—quick—back to the job, the ministry, back to "normal." Quick healing is not the tendency with emotional healing because the wounds can be deep. There is rarely a fast recovery. Life may, in fact, never go back to "normal," and that is actually ok. A new normal will happen, but it is likely that healing will be a slow process. Often while that sharp pain will dull, the scars will remain with you for the rest of your life.

It is ok to have scars, even scars on your heart. They show that you lived, that you loved. That there was pain, but that healing has also happened. When the skin grows back to form a scar, that skin is tougher, providing protection once again to an area that was once tender. Scars (even emotional ones) are a bit like a tattoo permanently branded on your flesh telling a story of something that hurt, but something that makes you who you are today, an identifying mark that leaves you a little bit stronger than you were in the past—a survivor.

So many Biblical texts embrace the idea of God as a healer of our wounds. Often these texts are looked at in the light of physical healing, but God is a holistic God who cares for the mind, soul, and body. He is, after all, the one who created intellect, emotions and our physical bodies. Even though His children live in a world that is tainted with sin and death, He longs to *heal*. Ultimate healing will of course happen in heaven, but physical and emotional healing can also happen (at least in part) on this side of eternity.

In Exodus 15:26 the Lord says, "I am the LORD, your healer." In Jeremiah 17:14 the prophet cries out, "Heal me, O LORD, and I shall be healed; save me, and I shall be saved." 1 Peter 2:24 says that "He personally carried our sins in his body on the cross so that we can be dead to sin and live for what is right. By His wounds you are healed" (NLT). Psalms 103:2-3 tells us, "Let all that I am praise the Lord; may I never forget the good things he does for me. He forgives all my sins and heals all my diseases" (NLT). Proverbs 3:7-8 says, "Fear the LORD and turn away from evil. It will be healing to your flesh and refreshment to your bones."

Jeremiah 30:17 also shows that God personally desires to heal wounds. "For I will restore health to you, and your wounds I will heal, declares the LORD." In Psalm 6:2 the psalmist turns to the Maker for healing, saying, "Have compassion on me, LORD, for I am weak. Heal me, LORD, for my bones are in agony" (NLT). Psalms 41:3 says, "The Lord nurses them when they are sick and restores them to health" (NLT).

Have any of these beautifully comforting verses struck a chord with you? Maybe jot them down on a note card and keep them somewhere where you look often as a reminder that ultimate healing (both physically and emotionally) comes from God. He longs to lavish His comfort and healing onto His beloved children.

> It is ok to have scars, even scars on your heart. They show that you lived, that you loved. That there was pain, but that healing has also happened. When the skin grows back to form a scar, that skin is tougher, providing protection once again to an area that was once tender. Scars (even emotional ones) are a bit like a tattoo permanently branded on your flesh telling a story of something that hurt, but something that makes you who you are today, an identifying mark that leaves you a little bit stronger than you were in the past—a survivor.

> "He heals the brokenhearted and binds up their wounds."
> —Psalm 147:3 (ESV)

A Father's Love

By Leah Nelson

AS I GREW up, and throughout most of my adult life, my relationship with my father could be described as…wondering. I had always wondered who and where he was; I often wondered if he was even alive. His continual silence caused me to question not only his existence, but also his love for me, and therefore; my own lovability. A natural result of neglect from one's parents is to question one's value. And so, I wondered. I wondered where he was and what was wrong with me.

My parents divorced when I was two years old due to a turbulent relationship surrounded by drugs. When I was a child, my mother filled my mind with every bad memory she had of my father. She told me that he was a violent schizophrenic who was suicidal, psychotic and abusive. Fear of my father began to form my view of him even though I did not know him. My mother also had a bad habit of lying, and I did not know what was true and what was not about anything or anyone. So, I was left to wonder. I wondered who this person was. Who was my father? Why was I afraid of him?

As I grew into my adolescence, I continued to wonder about my father, and it was awkward when I was asked about him. "I do not know where he lives or even if he is alive. I have not heard from him since I was two years old," was my most common response. I never talked about it unless questioned. The pain of all those neglected years grew with me and led me deeper into what felt like an abyss of loneliness. I wondered when, or if, I would see him again.

To my shock, tragedy led me to meet my father when I was 15 years old. On April 1, 1998, while I was at school, two young men went on a random shooting spree throughout southern Indiana and eastern Illinois. As these two men were on their murderous mission, they drove past my house, saw my mother's Camaro and decided they wanted it. They pulled up into the driveway, walked to the front door and knocked. Almost as soon as my mom answered, one of the men put a gun to her head and demanded to have the keys to her car.

As they demanded to have the keys, with a gun pressed to her head, my mom pleaded in a panic, "The keys are in the car. Please, please just take it. Please don't kill me!" My mom begged for her life in that surreal moment.

"Liar! Give us the keys or we will kill you!" the two young men responded in a mad rage.

"I am telling the truth! The keys are in the car…" She was shot dead, right there on our front porch. The men walked to the car to find that the keys were in the car and drove away with their prized possession.

> *She woke up in her daydreams*
> *Interrupted by her own shed blood*
> *The bullet shattered her unconscious*
> *And left her cold and alone*
> *Oh, they left her cold and alone…*

Five days later, I was hugging many adult strangers at my mom's visitation. Sadly, my mom was a partier and drug dealer, which meant she had many secrets that I am still discovering to this day. In her drug world, she knew people that I did not know which is why the service was filled with adults who were strangers to me. I was not paying attention to a lot of the people there; however, I distinctly remember a short, dark-skinned man who hugged me over and over. There were no words spoken, but his face was covered in tears. His weeping so heavy that he had a hard time maintaining his composure.

As he walked away, my aunt quickly rushed to my side and spoke into my ear with these unforgettable words, "Leah, do you see that man over there? That man is your father." I went numb and did not say anything. I just nodded my head and walked away, but I wondered. "Where did he come from? Where does he live? How did he know about this? Why is he so sad?"

I noticed that my dad was at the funeral and even the dinner afterwards the next day. I did not know how to act or what to do, but he used the opportunity to come and speak with my sister and me afterwards. I do not remember exactly what he, or I, said, but we exchanged words and decided to stay in touch through letters (this was before the Internet or cell phones). Even though I was glad to see him, I remember feeling confused about him and unsatisfied. The wondering in my heart had not been erased and my questions had not been answered; in fact, I wondered even more as I asked myself, "Where has he been my whole life? Where was he while my mom was out doing drugs? Where was he when stepdads were molesting me? Where was he?"

It was a day I would die to forget
And a moment I will always regret
To smell the scent of rushing tears
And to bury the pain of neglected years

Where were you in the darkest of times?
Where was the embrace to escape the lies?
I was drowning in the pouring rain
And I was dying from all my pain....

My father and I kept in touch through letters but as the months moved along, the letters became fewer and fewer and eventually nonexistent. I was so depressed and heavily into drug use that I could not keep up with it.

Fast forward 11 years to 2009. I was living in Joplin, Missouri, working for a prison ministry. About eight years prior, I experienced the radical transformation of coming to Christ. I came to Joplin to attend Bible college and decided to work and live there after graduation. As I was busy with work and ministry, I randomly received a message on MySpace from my stepmother, my father's wife. She informed me that my dad wanted to be in touch with me. Through this, I got my dad's email and phone number. To my joy, we started to talk again! I was exhilarated to feel pursued by my dad. At first, we talked nearly every day either through email or phone calls, but, as it had always been, the emails and the phone calls became fewer and fewer then faded away. I wondered why.

"Is there something wrong with me? Why would my own

father not pursue a relationship with me? What have I done? Why does he no longer speak to me?" I was devastated.

I did not hear from him again until 2014. My husband and I lived in Kenya when I received an email from my father to tell me that he had been diagnosed with colon cancer. From that moment forward, I received messages here and there that gave me updates about his condition. My dad also opened up a Facebook account where I could see pictures and find more updates. He endured much suffering under chemotherapy, had victories, successes and fallbacks. At times the cancer appeared to be gone, other times, it reappeared in different places, until eventually, it spread all throughout his abdomen. Despite the years of chemo and surgery, the cancer just never went away. We did not talk very much until things became quite serious with his health.

My husband, Phil, and I moved back to the United States in late 2015 in order to attend seminary at The Southern Baptist Theological Seminary in Louisville, Kentucky. In the late summer of 2017, my father and his wife traveled all the way to Kentucky to meet with Phil and me. It was a Saturday. We met at Panera Bread, my dad's favorite restaurant.

We had a good time together. It was the first time my dad had ever met Phil, and I was eight months pregnant with our son. Understandably, our conversations centered mostly around Phil and my dad learning about each other. We also talked about my pregnancy and how excited Phil and I were to be parents. Our conversations were light, but the topic of my dad's health was unavoidable.

"I've decided to stop chemo," he explained. "The doctor

warned me that the cancer will spread quickly, but the chemo is so terrible that I would rather have a short time to live, and really live, rather than live longer but suffer terribly." Tears filled his eyes.

I smiled and said, "That's a hard decision to make, but thank you for telling me, and I respect whatever decision you make." At that moment, I knew for sure that my father was going to die, but I wondered if he was saved.

> *Here comes the final goodbye*
> *As death steals the light of your eye*
> *My heart bleeds the fiercest tears,*
> *When you suffocate in your fears.*

From that moment until his death eight months later, I spoke with my dad nearly every week over the phone. He came down to visit several times after I gave birth to my son, Emet. I am so happy that I have pictures of him and Emet together; Emet was just a baby and will not remember meeting his grandfather. We also traveled north to see my dad. Each time I saw him, he was weaker, sicker, more frail and tired. My dad was always happy, optimistic, kind and very gentle. He was a quiet man who put a lot of thought behind each word.

Over time, my dad explained to me that he had been reading "lots of Scripture," and had a meeting with a pastor to talk about death. He told me that he had given his life to Christ and that he believed it was God's will for him to go home to heaven. I no longer wondered about his salvation. He also apologized for his neglect in the past, and we came to peace.

Eight days before my dad passed away, he called me. He could only speak in slow whispers. With heavy breath, he said to me, "Leah, I know I sound different, but you sound the same." He laughed a little; he was always so happy. Then he said, "Leah, my daughter, I love you. Please know that I love you. I wanted to hear your voice."

I said, "I love you dad, and I will see you again. I will see you in heaven."

He replied, "Yes, Leah, I will see you there. I love you." The next day he fell into a coma, and he died seven days later, on April 21, 2018. He was 67 years old.

> *Even though I walk through the valley of the shadow of death,*
> *I will fear no evil, for you are with me;*
> *your rod and your staff, they comfort me.*
> *-Psalm 23:4 (NIV)*

My son and I, along with my father-in-law and mother-in-law, traveled north for the visitation and the funeral. Phil was gone for military training (he joined the military as a chaplain…I know, we go through many life changes) and could not go with us. The drive was about seven hours and seemed to last forever before we finally arrived in the cold northern Indiana city. I was nervous as we approached the funeral home. I dreaded seeing my father's body in the coffin. I actually had not cried before the visitation because I had convinced myself that it wasn't really that hard. "I have dealt with so much death in my life, and this isn't as bad as my mom's death. I've got this, I will be fine," I told myself. All that changed as soon as I walked in the door of the funeral home.

Everything hit me all at once. I thought to myself, "It's over, it's all over. The wondering, the questioning, the pursuing of a relationship—it's over…but it just started. I just started a relationship with him, and now I have to finish it. I don't know how. God, help me." I cried very hard. I had just started the relationship that I had longed for my whole life, only to have it taken away by death. It all seemed so sudden.

The truth is, no matter how someone dies, whether quickly or slowly, death is sudden, and no one is ever prepared for it. Death is sudden because the person is there one minute, and then is gone the next. Everything changes after that split second. Death is hard because it is the ultimate separation. You cannot be more separated from a person than when they die, and that separation is final. Nothing can be added to that life; what has been done is done and there is no return. Such things are hard to accept. It is hard to move on after someone dies.

I cried a lot at the visitation and the funeral. I let all my grief out. It was hard, but I felt like I did get the closure that I needed. I had a good time visiting with family members, and they loved seeing Emet.

It was a difficult month after my father's death. I learned to close the door to the relationship I had always wanted and had finally obtained. I accepted that it was God's will for my dad to go home, just as my dad said it was.

Your life was never mine to give,
Nor mine to take away.
Your life belongs to the Lord,
And it was His will to turn the page.

My greatest comfort was knowing that my dad gave his life to Christ. In fact, the pastor with whom my dad regularly met preached the Gospel and shared my dad's testimony at his funeral. My dad's death and funeral glorified God. I never thought I would see such a thing in my life and I truly could not ask for anything more. I will see my dad again, and it will be the perfect reunion.

I made peace with my dad; he is in eternal glory. I do not have to wonder anymore.

A Psalm for Reflection

Psalm 147

Praise the LORD.
How good it is to sing praises to our God,
how pleasant and fitting to praise him!
The LORD builds up Jerusalem;
he gathers the exiles of Israel.
He heals the brokenhearted
and binds up their wounds.
He determines the number of the stars
and calls them each by name.
Great is our Lord and mighty in power;
his understanding has no limit.
The LORD sustains the humble
but casts the wicked to the ground.
Sing to the Lord with grateful praise;
make music to our God on the harp.
He covers the sky with clouds;
he supplies the earth with rain
and makes grass grow on the hills.
He provides food for the cattle
and for the young ravens when they call.
His pleasure is not in the strength of the horse,
nor his delight in the legs of the warrior;
the LORD delights in those who fear him,
who put their hope in his unfailing love.
Extol the LORD, Jerusalem;
praise your God, Zion.
He strengthens the bars of your gates

Permission to Mourn

and blesses your people within you.
He grants peace to your borders
and satisfies you with the finest of wheat.
He sends his command to the earth;
his word runs swiftly.
He spreads the snow like wool
and scatters the frost like ashes.
He hurls down his hail like pebbles.
Who can withstand his icy blast?
He sends his word and melts them;
he stirs up his breezes, and the waters flow.
He has revealed his word to Jacob,
his laws and decrees to Israel.
He has done this for no other nation;
they do not know his laws.
Praise the Lord (NIV).

CHAPTER FOUR

The Crown Does Not Put on a Show

"The friend who can be silent with us in a moment of despair or confusion, who can stay with us in an hour of grief and bereavement, who can tolerate not knowing, not curing, not healing and face with us the reality of our powerlessness, that is a friend who cares."

—Henri J. M. Nouwen (Out of Solitude:Three Meditations on the Christian life)

Like so many people, I was pulled into binge watching the Netflix series *The Crown*. The episode "Aberfan" touched me as it brilliantly illustrates the complexities of grieving and comforting a community in mourning. The episode highlights the tragedy that took place in Aberfan, Wales, on October, 21 1966. An over abundance of rain caused a coal waste tip (a giant mound of debris left as part of a mining operation) to collapse, creating a landslide that engulfed parts of a mining village.[6] The Pantglas Junior School took the brunt of the landslide resulting in the deaths of 116 children and 28 adults.

The town was understandably devastated. The episode follows Prime Minister Harold Wilson who rushes to the scene of the disaster. He later encourages Queen Elizabeth II to also go and

Permission to Mourn

visit the grief-stricken community. The queen hesitates and says that her presence usually makes situations more complicated "What precisely would you have me do?" she asks the prime minister.

"Comfort people," he responds.

"Put on a show?" says Olivia Coleman, who plays the queen. "The Crown does not do that."

"I did not say put on a show," the prime minister quietly responds. "I said comfort people."

It is a moving episode showing many different people shaken to their core and their varied responses to loss and tragedy. In the episode, the queen continues to avoid traveling to Aberfan and decides not to attend the mass funeral where the majority of the children's coffins are buried in a mass grave laid out in the shape of a cross. When public pressure finally pushes the queen to visit the mining village herself, she later shares with the prime minister what kept her most from going. It was not her fear of being overwhelmed by emotion, but her fear of being unable to show genuine emotion as she often found herself unable to shed tears when others around her wept.

"I have known for some time that there is something wrong with me," she says to the prime minister.

"Not wrong," the prime minister replies.

"Deficient, then," says the queen.

"We cannot be everything to everyone and still be true to ourselves," the prime minister wisely responds.

The queen felt inadequate to be a comfort in a difficult situation, so initially she avoided the messy situation. However, when she did go, her presence was enough. She could not fix the problem—no one could. But her physically being present in the village, to share the problem was enough to bring comfort. The episode ends with a postscript saying that those close to the queen say one of her greatest regrets is her delayed response to the disaster and that she has since returned to the village more times than any other member of the royal family.[7]

While it is important to note that the show *The Crown* is a drama set around historical events and not a documentary, the episode does a good job of reflecting how complicated responses to grief and tragedy can be. It shows how easy it is to feel inadequate. It shows how tempting it can be to stay away, afraid that you will make things worse. It demonstrates how easy it is to fear doing the wrong thing when trying to comfort and how much of a comfort the basic ministry of simply being present can really be.

It is easy to ask yourself, "What can I do? The situation is too much—too many questions and not enough answers. What can I even say?" So often we stay away in fear, afraid that we will end up saying the wrong thing, because often we do. As much as you want to fix or take away the pain of death, it is impossible to do so. Even in instances in Scripture when an individual was raised miraculously from the dead, the person eventually passed away again. This is the fate of mankind. We are mortal. The nature of this world is that everything, no matter how sweet, is temporary and always will be this side of eternity.

As much as we long to "fix" problems and eradicate pain, it is beyond human control to bring a loved one back. Words, even words from Scripture, can often feel cheap or empty. Scripture itself is far from empty but verses (often taken out of context) and thrown at someone in pain can cause a person who is in the midst of grief to *deflect* comfort instead of letting it sink into the heart. Promises in the Bible and favorite verses, while true and comforting, too often become a way of shutting down conversation and not allowing a person to process pain. Too often pat answers, like "They are in a better place now," or "God works out everything for good," while technically true are not necessarily helpful for a person who just needs to cry out and express hurt. Those who are grieving need space to do just that. Let the Holy Spirit guide your words to a person in pain—often saying less is more.

> As much as we long to "fix" problems and eradicate pain, it is beyond human control to bring a loved one back. Words, even words from Scripture, can often feel cheap or empty. Scripture itself is far from empty but verses (often taken out of context) and thrown at someone in pain can cause a person who is in the midst of grief to deflect comfort instead of letting it sink into the heart.

People often unconsciously quote familiar platitudes for their own comfort, trying desperately to make sense of tragedy. So what should we do? Often the answer is—just sit. Make a cup of tea and sit with your friend, letting them say as little or as much as they are comfortable with. Send a "Just checking in on you or praying for you today" text and then actually pray for them. Seek to let the lack of words—not the abundance of advice—create a safe environment for processing and mourning. Don't avoid; just be present.

Eliphaz, Bildad, and Zophar sat on the ground with Job for seven days and seven nights after Job lost his children, his wealth and his physical health. Job's friends heard about his trouble and travelled to be with him. They saw him—and the pain had so affected Job that his friends did not even recognize him. When the trio of friends saw Job from afar, they wept aloud, tore the very clothes on their bodies and sprinkled dust on their hair. They sat in stunned silence waiting for Job to speak. "No one said a word," Job 2:13 says, "for they saw that his suffering was very great." In their silence the three friends seemed to bring Job comfort. Then they spoke, desperate to make some kind of sense of the obvious tragedy. The friends felt compelled to give some kind of advice, some answers to the "why" questions that burned in everyone's mind. They no longer simply sat. They no longer just listened. They jumped in with human logic and answers, and when they did, they ceased to be a comfort.

It is human nature to long to speak. One of the first things Eliphaz says to Job is, "who can keep from speaking?" (Job 4:2) So Job's friends jumped in with their assessment of the situation before them. "Who that was innocent, has ever perished?" (Job 4:7) "Those who sow trouble reap it" (Job 4:8b NIV). "Can a mortal be more righteous than God?" (Job 4:17 NIV) "But if I were you, I would appeal to God" (Job 5:8 NIV). "Blessed is the man whom God corrects; so do not despise the discipline of the Almighty. For he wounds but he also binds up" (Job 5:17-18 NIV). "We have examined this, and it is true. So hear it and apply it to yourself" (Job 5:27 NIV) In summary—all of this must be your fault somehow. Here is what I would do if I were in your place. We know what we are saying is right so apply it to your life.

How did Job respond to these words of "comfort"? He responds with some pretty strong words of his own, coming (understandably) from a place of raw emotion. "For the despairing man there should be kindness from his friend," Job says in Job 6:14 (NASB). "Now you too have proved to be of no help; you see something dreadful and are afraid" (Job 6:21 NIV). "What do your arguments prove?" (Job 6:25b NIV) Job's friends' responses and attempts at comfort came, not from a place of genuine love, but of *fear*. The tragedy that was unfolding before them through the life of Job did not fit with their predetermined, carefully boxed up and categorized ideas of how life should work—mainly that people who did evil suffered and the righteous prospered. In their minds, a good God would not allow this level of catastrophe to touch the life of a righteous person; therefore, Job must not be as righteous as he claimed.

On and on Job and his friends go—chapter upon chapter, of speech after speech, follow one debate after another as Job clings to his innocence and his friends grow more and more frustrated with him and him with them.

Then God speaks—silencing them all. And what was God's response to the many, many words of "wisdom" from Job's friends? "I am angry with you and your two friends," He speaks to Eliphaz, the first friend to break the initial silence Job 42:7 (NIV). "You have not spoken the truth about me as my servant Job has." The three friends are commanded to make a sacrifice for themselves and to ask Job to pray for them. "My servant Job will pray for you, and I will accept his prayer and not deal with you according to your folly" (Job 42:8 NIV).

Job forgave his "comforters" and their hurtful presumptions and *after* Job prayed and forgave his friends God *once again* made him prosperous giving him twice as much as he had before. There is nothing black and white about grief and tragedy. It is often a whole lot of grey. We cannot see the whole picture this side of eternity, and frequently it just plain does not make sense. Why the multiple miscarriages when someone is longing for a child? Why the car accident weeks before a high school graduation? Why do some fiancés end up cutting wedding planning short to instead plan the funeral of the person they had dreamed about spending the rest of their life with? Why are some people asked to walk through so much pain?

Grief does not fit into carefully categorized boxes. There is no easy ten-step, foolproof process for working through it. But, that does not mean that we should not attempt to take steps towards healing. Even the famous five steps of grief proposed by Elisabeth Kubler-Ross in her book *On Death and Dying*, while helpful at points, fall a bit flat as a cure-all for working through personal grief. This is probably, in part, because the steps (denial, anger, bargaining, depression and acceptance) were developed after studying terminally ill patients in the *process* of dying, not those processing the death of a loved one.[8] With this information in mind, the steps actually make more sense. It is more likely, for

Permission to Mourn

example, for someone who is facing death herself to try to make bargains with God than it is for someone whose loved one has already passed away to bargain. Will there be anger and denial when someone dies? It is very likely that there will be. Will there be depression and acceptance? It is very probable that there will be days of depression and also days of acceptance. There can also be days that involve both periods of acceptance and periods of depression within the very same hour because grief is a complex creature.

So what do we do? We go. We weep. We mourn. We make mistakes, but we learn from those mistakes and grow in our ability to be a better instrument of comfort when the next opportunity arises. What we should *not* do is avoid, wait and give pat answers because we are afraid.

> "Rejoice with those who rejoice; mourn with those who mourn."
> —Romans 12:15 (NIV)

Fading Photographs

By Sarah Price

THERE ARE TWO phone calls I will never forget. Some moments freeze in your memory and stick. The slightest push sends them back into one's mind with the force of the initial memory. In 2013, I was teaching a class in Kenya and living with relatives in a home my grandpa had built many years before. Every Sunday evening, I'd call home and check in with everyone. I'd pace the kitchen floor, carefully stepping on each tile around in a circle, as I chatted about the class I was teaching and how everyone was doing at home.

Then, early one Wednesday morning, just as I ought to be waking up; my phone rang. No one really knew my number except my parents. I snuck out of my room to keep from waking up my cousin and went downstairs. It was my parents. My grandma, who'd been in a car accident four months earlier, had passed away. I froze. The last time I'd seen Grandma was at Christmas right before I left for Kenya. She and Grandpa had been in a car accident when we were on our way to Florida for our annual Christmas visit. They were probably on the way to the Dollar Store to pick up some last minute presents for us kids when a car turned into their lane and hit them. Grandma likely panicked, hit the gas and slammed their car into a telephone pole. Or something like that.

The details were a little difficult to gather. Grandpa walked away with a few cracked ribs, but Grandma's leg was shattered. She suffered a stroke due to the stress of the accident shortly after reaching the hospital. She then floated in and out of reality for the next four months. When I visited at Christmas, I went up to her hospital bed. Her leg was covered in a metal cage to try to give her brittle bones the chance to heal. She acted like she knew who we were, but she asked me to get her the plates from the cabinet. As she touched my hands, she thought I'd given her the tomatoes to slice for the Christmas dinner salad. After a short visit, we left. I suspected, but didn't know, this visit would be my last with her.

I froze, in stunned silence, after hanging up the phone. Here I was thousands of miles away with a class to teach in just a few hours. There was no option of going home for the funeral. My ticket was already booked for April 1st, and I still had a month left of my class to teach. I heard the gentle tread of footsteps down the stairs. My uncle had heard the phone and knew something was wrong. He came down to check on me, so I told him what I'd just heard. He responded with a hug and asked me what my favorite memories with Grandma were. It helped to know that someone else wanted to know. The shock slowly faded and gave way to memories, but the ache didn't go away. In fact, it came back now just remembering.

Every time we went to visit Grandma and Grandpa in Florida, we would have at least one picnic at the park with a giant wooden play-castle. The adults would set up the food, and the cousins would run off to the playground. We would chase each other all over the park. Then we'd head back over to the picnic tables and have sandwiches and chips. Grandma loved picnics. Even when we got too big to fit in the playground, we would still go to the same park for a picnic lunch and a walk. Grandma always made sure that there were ice cream sandwiches and fudgsicles for dessert, whenever we came to visit. She loved cooking meals for her family, so I guess it was fitting that the last time I saw her, she thought she was preparing Christmas dinner.

The hardest part of losing Grandma, though, wasn't the initial shock, or even going to class and continuing with my responsibilities in Kenya. The hardest part was seeing the pictures from the funeral service and hearing everyone's stories of bonding afterward. I missed that. I wasn't there. Even still, I can't name exactly what happened during that time; but I remember hearing about all my aunts, uncles and cousins hanging out with my parents and siblings at my grandparents' house on Crescent Drive. There were stories and memories from that time that I missed. I simply couldn't be there. Grief hits differently when you miss the community of grievers. It made me all the more thankful for my uncle who took the time to sit with me and ask about my memories.

This wasn't the only call. The exact date has faded from memory now, but two years later, I got another call. I was working in a data entry position, and my phone rang. I glanced at the number and saw it was my dad. I quickly noted that I would be away from my desk and headed to the hallway to answer the phone. I leaned up against the file cabinet and answered the call. Grandpa passed away, almost exactly two years after his wife. I shrunk to the floor and tried to hear what my dad was saying. I knew Grandpa hadn't been well. He had moved into an assisted living facility after Grandma passed away. His Alzheimer's had progressed to the point where he couldn't care for himself and in-home care wasn't really an option either. I knew he had been worse lately, too ill to go to the dining hall for dinner; but still the shock hit like a wave. There was no room for tears; no uncle coming downstairs this time. I choked back the memories, and went back to work. Scan the incoming email, follow the procedure, forward it on. Scan the incoming email, follow the procedure, forward it on. I suppose, looking back, I could have gone to my boss and asked to go home early; but I wasn't ready to talk to anyone. Scan the incoming email, follow the procedure, forward it on. There was something comforting in the redundant and boring.

This time I was able to fly down for the service. I was able to be there for the memory making, to be present with the grievers. My sister was the one stuck this time. She had just left a few months before to start a new life on a different side of the world. You can't always afford to hop the globe for a memorial service. As I sat in Grandma and Grandpa's old house on Crescent Drive, beautiful memories flooded back to me. When we were little, my sister and I loved piling up on Grandpa's knee for a hug or a story or a just because. Of course, one does not stay little forever, and there came a time when Grandpa's knees just couldn't manage us both at once. So, we would race to see who could get there first. There were no favorites. He'd just take whichever one of us got there first. Then my sister got sneaky. When I'd get there first, she'd tell me someone was looking for me. I'd reluctantly hop off Grandpa's lap to go find them, and she'd hop up. Grandpa would laugh and laugh to see us both trying to find a way to be the one who got there first. Grandpa also loved his fruitcake. Every time we'd come to visit, he'd go to the dollar store and get a bag of Hershey miniatures. Those were what he called his fruitcake savers. He'd put those out, so us grandkids would leave his fruitcake alone. I never told him that I wasn't a fan of fruitcake, because I got chocolate out of the deal.

Honestly though that call was the second time I'd lost Grandpa. The first time I really felt the loss was when I was preparing for my wedding in 2014. Grandpa was already in the assisted living home at that point, and I felt as though inviting him for our wedding would be too much for him. He just didn't know what was going on around him anymore. I felt that bringing him up for the wedding would put him so far out of his comfort zone that his health would deteriorate faster. Instead, we chose to visit him after our honeymoon. I wrote him a letter that I never mailed and tucked it away in the invitation with his name that I never sent. Not everyone agreed, but I just couldn't send it. I didn't want to cause more confusion or hurt if he knew about the wedding but couldn't come. It was better that way, or at least I think it was. Some days I still wonder. During our visit, I kept walking over to the wall where my aunt had carefully hung and labeled all of the kids and grandkid's pictures. I'd point to my picture on the wall with Eric and re-explain to Grandpa how I knew him. At lunch, they served pumpkin pie, his least favorite; but he smiled, added sugar, and ate it with the biggest smile on his face. I guess that's the benefit of Alzheimer's. You enjoy new favorites every day.

Both my grandparents lived a full life. They loved their four girls, their sons-in-law and grandkids. Going through their house, I got to read letters my Grandma's little third graders wrote thanking her for being their teacher. We also found the old worn copy of their daily devotional which always showed up at the table twice a day. Whoever was at the meal always heard the Scriptures being read. We got to see traces of their lives. Still, there is an ache there from love. There was something soothing about going to Bushnell two summers ago and seeing their headstone. Grandma on one side; Grandpa on the other. Buried together. Best friends for nearly 60 earthly years. Still, I wish they'd known my Eric. I wish they'd met my little Lucy. I wanted them there for our wedding, and my sister's, and my brother's. And yet... People try to soothe by saying that someone lived a full life; and while I think we ought to try to live well, the pain of love does not lessen with time. The pain of love pulls us to be vulnerable with others. It forces us to know that love does not exist for separation. We were not created to be separated from relationships. Grief does fade, but more like the fading of a photograph. Still etched in the surface of our soul is the likeness of another who touched us.

A Psalm for Reflection

Psalm 6

O LORD, rebuke me not in your anger,
nor discipline me in your wrath.
Be gracious to me, O LORD, for I am languishing;
heal me, O LORD, for my bones are troubled.
My soul also is greatly troubled.
But you, O LORD— how long?
Turn, O LORD, deliver my life;
save me for the sake of your steadfast love.
For in death there is no remembrance of you;
in Sheol who will give you praise?
I am weary with my moaning;
every night I flood my bed with tears;
I drench my couch with my weeping.
My eye wastes away because of grief;
it grows weak because of all my foes.
Depart from me, all you workers of evil,
for the LORD has heard the sound of my weeping.
The LORD has heard my plea;
the LORD accepts my prayer.
All my enemies shall be ashamed and greatly troubled;
they shall turn back and be put to shame in a moment.

CHAPTER FIVE

Finding Solace in Structure

> "Some people think that having ash on your forehead is ridiculous. But I am neither ashamed nor afraid because the ashes remind me that I have to someday pass away and reunite with my creator"
>
> —Walter Buns

This week is the start of Lent, a practice I've never chosen to participate in before but one I am leaning into for the first time this Easter season. I am less than a week in and I am already learning so much— mostly that it is hard. Using the book *Every Broken Thing: A Lent and Holy Week Guide to Answering Ecclesiastes* by Erin Hicks Moon, my stressed soul is already finding a sweet release in allowing myself to take time out to meditate on the more complex issues of life. Dust, ashes, death, dashed hopes and deep sorrow. These themes swirl around Lent as preparations are made to remember the death of Christ and then celebrate the life-giving hope of His resurrection.

In the past, I had a tendency to see Lent simply as a time to give something up. It felt stiff, traditional and even a bit ritualistic. But, the more I have learned about Lent; the more I see its value as a time to pause, remember, meditate and even mourn. In Erin Hick Moon's *Lent Primer*, she explains this idea beautifully when she writes, "Now that I've experienced the rhythms of the calendar and liturgy for a few years, it's given me several gifts; the first gift is movement. Within the days portioned out during the year, I'm given space and guardrails to experience certain feelings. During Lent, no one is asking me to be happy and cherry: we're supposed to be somber, we're supposed to be introspective. The church calendar gives me markers throughout the year to say: I can hold sadness here. I can hold joy here. It pushes me through emotions that I might otherwise get stuck in, gently urging me forward with its cadence."[9]

Often solace can be found in structure. When our carefully planned out worlds start to crumble in, falling back on traditions can be a comfort because traditions often stand the test of time and have survived generations for a reason. Traditions bring with them a sense of stability and that stability can be an anchor to a weary heart navigating through pathways of pain. Traditions are often built around doing something, holding something physical, visiting a monument or singing a familiar mantra. Traditions can add constancy in a world that feels ever changing. Maybe this is part of the reason that God told the Israelites to set up Ebenezers, memorials and altars. He commanded His people to observe many different feasts, festivals and days of remembrance—times specifically set aside to remember and recall. Stone memorials were set up as reminders. Specific phrases, songs and Psalms were to be repeated throughout the calendar year. When a leader, like

Moses or King David, died there was a set number of days that the community set aside to mourn. These set times and traditions were, and often still are, an important part of Jewish culture and calendar. Lent can play a similar role of adding structure and space for Christians today to take time out to process, mourn and remember.

In a world of next day shipping, Instagram, instant messaging and instant coffee, slowness is rarely seen as a virtue. It is easy to want the quick fix so that life can just move on again; but if you look in the pages of scripture that is rarely how things work. We often want to skip the 40 years in the wilderness, I mean really, who has that kind of time? Waiting is so often seen in a negative light not a positive one. But, the lessons learned in the wilderness can be some of the most character shaping lessons that God has for his children. Lessons that cannot be learned anywhere else. If we are truly going to follow in our savior's earthly footsteps, then the wilderness is a stop that cannot be passed over. Instead of seeking a detour, maybe it is time to make time to sit for 40 days in the midst of the dust and pain that accompanies the wilderness. Will it be a joyful time? There may be joy mixed in with the silence and

> In a world of next day shipping, Instagram, instant messaging and instant coffee, slowness is rarely seen as a virtue. It is easy to want the quick fix so that life can just move on again; but if you look in the pages of scripture that is rarely how things work.

pondering, but the balance of stopping— truly stopping—will allow needed time to mourn and jumpstart the process of healing.

We tend to be an overloaded culture in this modern age that works long hours and provides short maternity leaves. Many employers are reluctant to give days off and some professors can be unwilling to bend the syllabus even in times of death. This back-breaking pace does not leave much room for reflection or mourning. Maybe we can squeeze in a 4-hour stop in the wilderness (ok let's be real, a 40 minute stop), but that is all this busy culture allows. This means if you truly want time and space to heal it is likely that you will have to choose to be counter-cultural, at times, in your approach to healing. Maybe a professor will refuse to bend, and an assignment might get sacrificed in the process. Maybe there will be a need to switch jobs if an employer refuses to allow time off but more likely people will understand. Most people have faced the pain of death themselves and, when asked, will be accommodating. We each have just one life and at times it is worth sacrificing a job or a grade in order to take time for mental and emotional health.

Because there are not often times naturally set aside for processing grief, it can be helpful to intentionally seek to create your own traditions or lean into existing practices that can help provide space to sit with hard feelings. The physical four seasons can even act as a time to reflect, contemplate life, death, growth and new beginnings as do birthdays and anniversaries. Do not simply let times and seasons pass by passively. What do they have to teach? How has the year without your loved one grown or changed you? Of course, this can be hard, but often there is a softness that accompanies reflection on loss.

Like a seed buried in the ground waiting for the growth of spring—grief can also be a seed that brings with it new compassion, new love, new perspective and even a new hope. If we choose to only wallow in the negative, these fruits will not have a chance to grow. Pain and loss have purpose. Of course, we would rather they had not happened in the first place; but when we allow God to pen the pages of our lives new growth will take place. Looking back—it is often the parts that were the hardest (the parts we wouldn't even wish on our worst enemy) that tend to grow and change us the most. This is why we need each season of life. This is why we cannot fixate only on the hard, the pain and the wrong. If we do, we could miss out on the ways that God wants to grow us. We could miss out on the new things that He has for us—the season that comes after the sting of the snow.

I'll never forget the Easter Sunday that I spent in Kenya sitting completely numb under towering acacia trees. A sudden change in circumstances had made it clear that the team I was a part of needed to leave the children's home, where I had been volunteering for nearly a year, and go back to our home countries. The writing had been on the wall, but I never expected to have to pack my belongings in the space of a day and attempt to say goodbye to the children who had been under my care knowing that it was very likely that I would never see those precious faces again, this side of heaven. It was a traumatic parting to say the least, and yet somehow there was a sense of peace knowing that a door was now closed. But, it was a door that was supposed to close. As hard as it was, God made it clear that a beautiful season was coming to the end, and it was time to let go.

Permission to Mourn

As I drove off on the back of a pikipiki (motorcycle) the wind mixed with the tears that leaked from the corners of my eyes. I wondered, "what now God?" It was not supposed to end like this. I loved those kids like they were my own and yet; it was no longer my responsibility to care for them. Letting go of something you love deeply, hurts deeply. That Easter service I had a hard time celebrating. Wounds were too fresh. I ended up at a friend of a friend's house invited to an annual outdoor missionary gathering in celebration of Easter. The day was a blur, but I'll never forget the time of testimony. A lady stood at one point to share a story. Her story was about the loss of a dream and how sometimes when a good thing has ended we want to keep it so badly that we try to replant a dead branch thinking it will bear fruit. But, when a branch has fallen off a tree; nature must take its course. The branch will decompose and eventually new life can spring from what was once dead. If we just cling to that dead branch, what life can come of it? Yet, as humans, we want to continue to cling to what was once good and alive instead of letting go and letting time and nature do the work of regeneration producing new growth and life.

That illustration helped me begin to let go. Sure it took years of struggling, recurring bad dreams and a lot of prayer and forgiveness, but God took the dream that I thought was going to be a long-term dream and gave a new ministry and new dreams that I never expected. That is the type of God He is. Yes, He allows pain; but the pain has purpose. We see a slice of what He is doing in and around us, but He sees the bigger picture. He sees the seasons, the ebbs and the flows that will touch us between now and eternity. He does bring us through the wilderness, but it is for our good, for His glory and for the good of those around us.

Sometimes in life you will need to mourn the loss of a loved one. Sometimes it will be the loss of a dream or even the loss of innocence. You might find yourself mourning that life has just changed and that change can be difficult. Whatever you find yourself mourning, I encourage you to look for those natural times just to reflect, ponder and take time to learn the lessons that need to be learned in that season because it is likely that when you give yourself the time and space to do so; the wilderness will make you better and you will likely walk away with ways that you can comfort others in their journey and search for hope in this often broken world of ashes and dust.

"To every thing there is a season, and a time to every purpose under heaven: A time to be born and a time to die: a time to plant and a time to pluck up that which is planted. A time to kill, and a time to heal: a time to break down and a time to build up." —Ecclesiastes 3:1-3 (KJV)

In the Process of Becoming

By Ann-Marie Ferry

I LAY ON my side in bed during the twilight hours. Poking my stomach, I waited for a response, a kick, a roll, something. "Please child, just give me a sign that you are okay," I whispered.

Groggily I made my way to the bathroom, in a half awake, half asleep stupor. As I looked up, it was as if I had never seen my face before. A memory as real and vivid as the bathroom I stood in came to mind. I was reminded of a time during my college years when I foresaw the terrible future coming towards me and remembered thinking that it was the worst thing that could happen. And recalling the moments that followed (when I knew the terrible thing had come true) I realized, "The worst has happened and I'm still here."

I prayed as I stood facing the mirror. I prayed that God would bring my child to adulthood, just like I had prayed many times before, starting with the day I knew I was pregnant with him. This was my second pregnancy. My eldest, his big sister, lay asleep in a white crib in the room just beyond the bathroom wall. Only 13 months old, she was still just a baby herself. My pregnancy with her had been riddled with problems, and I was painfully aware that her safe and healthy delivery had been something of a miracle. This pregnancy with my son had not been as difficult thus far, but in the weeks leading up to this Monday; I had begun to have spotting and contractions. Twenty-four hours had now passed since the last time I felt a kick. Leaving early for work, I determined that I would head up to the obstetrics floor at the hospital where I worked before I started my shift that morning.

"Nothing," I thought to myself as I pulled up to the hospital. Surely this is nothing. I am probably just being overly cautious. The sterile white corridors that I was accustomed to walking were quiet that morning. The usual hub of patients, stretchers, nurses, doctors, and wheelchairs had not yet begun. I arrived on the second floor a half hour prior to my shift starting. Taking a deep breath, I pressed the buzzer to be let into the OB unit.

I stepped onto the unit and entered a whirlwind of apprehension and waiting. The nurses began with a Doppler to locate the heartbeat. Silence was all we heard. Continuing with a fetal heart monitor, we were struck again with the echo of silence where a heartbeat should be found. Three ultrasound techs entered the room like the masked doctors of the black plague, a last hope mixed with a grave reality. As they left one said, "We will give our report to your doctor." Their grim faces gave little hope, but I would not let go of that morsel of hope. After all, that is what mothers do.

My husband, Jon, now sat beside me. We waited. My obstetrician entered the room. Choosing a chair near the door, he sat down. "So, what do you think?" he asked. A little confused, I said, "We are just trying to not freak out until we have reason to." "The pregnancy isn't going to continue," he said. "There isn't a heartbeat."

Just then a young nurse piped in, "They hadn't been told. We were waiting on you."

With a look of horror on his face he apologized, "I am sorry. I didn't realize. I didn't want you to find out that way." As he continued to speak, the tears that had been held back the last two hours began to flow and the only thing that ran through my mind was, "It is well, it is well with my soul."

The doctor gave us two options: go home for the day and then come back to be induced tomorrow or stay and be induced right away. Horrified by the thought of having to prolong my emotional pain and by the thought of scarring my especially young daughter with the tears that at this point would not stop flowing, I chose to stay and be induced that day.

Once in the delivery room I removed the scrubs I would have normally worn for work and put on a hospital gown. I was no longer an expectant mother coming into work to take care of patients. I was instead a patient mourning the loss of her child. The induction began around 10:00 a.m. "The induction may take quite a bit longer than your first delivery" (which had been 12 hours) the nurse informed me. With this in mind, Jon and I settled in as the contractions began.

As the contractions came and went, we discussed the only thing we could at that point, what to name our baby boy. Just days earlier we had started to settle on Kuyper and now it seemed it would not be right to name him anything else.

The contractions became more and more intense as time passed. As I went into transitional labor my contractions felt more and more like the worst cramps imaginable yet somehow entirely unimaginable. The pain was so intense my entire body shook from it. I gripped the bed screaming and crying. The pain was cathartic, letting me act on the outside how I felt on the inside. Jon nervously paced the room. The pain became even more intense, and I screamed and cried even louder. Then the pain began to release as his head crowned. The nurse called the doctor as I lay back and closed my eyes. I was drained, but I was almost done.

I lay there half asleep in exhaustion. I could hardly believe that when the day had begun everything was "alright." Now I was delivering my dead son. And yet, he was still with me in body. I would still get to look on the face of the beautiful little creature who had lit up my world for twenty-three glorious weeks. Then I heard the doctor's voice as he came into the room. With two nurses and the doctor ready, I began to push. I pushed and pushed for what seemed an exceptionally long time. "Is this going anywhere?" I wondered. "Why don't you go ahead and rest a moment?" the doctor instructed. As my body relaxed, I felt Kuyper's head coming down. "He's coming!" I alerted the staff who were now turned away. "Are you pushing?" someone asked. "No!" I replied. Within moments the doctor had guided Kuyper, his intact amniotic sac and the placenta out all at once.

I began to cry. Jon took my hand. I turned my face toward him, and we wept together for our sweet boy, who never got to take his first breath. As the nurses were wiping off Kuyper, the doctor turned his attention to me. With tears welling up in his eyes he looked at me and said, "I want you to know that this was not your fault. There was nothing that you could have done. If you would have come in a few days ago the result would have been the same."

I looked up at the clock. Kuyper's labor and delivery took seven and a half hours. Seven and a half hours of pain and tears that I would not trade for anything. Just like mothers of living babies would not trade their suffering for anything because it brought them their bundle of joy. I too would not trade my pain for anything because it gave me a chance to hold my child in my arms, even if for a short time, and the chance to give him a proper burial. I would do it all again because I love him.

The next five hours were a blur. My mom showed up, exhausted from her long day of driving from Indiana. She came in and gave me a hug. She must have thought that I was still early on in labor because she did not notice the baby wrapped in the blanket that lay between my crossed legs as I sat up in the bed. When she saw him, her eyes welled up and she asked to hold him. Throughout the course of the evening Jon, my mom, my mother-in-law and I took turns holding and rocking sweet Kuyper. We talked about his name and who he looked like. We cried mostly. And in between our sobs we would try to speak words of comfort and encouragement to each other.

Eventually, after I had eaten my weight in enchiladas, hospital food and cookies the nurse helped me get out of bed so I could put on my pajamas. I looked down at my now flabby, postpartum belly. I could hardly comprehend that I was no longer pregnant. I could have sworn I felt him moving, but it was just my uterus contracting.

"You can come and get him at 9:30," I informed the nurse but 9:30 p.m. came and went and I just could not give Kuyper up. Every motherly instinct in me told me to hold him, protect him and to never let him go. How could I ever do the impossible? As time passed, we continued to take pictures, and to hold and rock our dear Kuyper. The nurse came in to take his handprints and footprints. We were all physically and emotionally worn out. A little before 10:30 p.m. I asked Jon to get out the video camera and I sang my sweet baby boy to eternal sleep. "Before the Throne of God Above" and "You are My Sunshine," the songs he had heard every night of his pregnancy, came out in squeaks and sobs. I put on the call light for the nurse. Wrapping him in a blanket I handed her my little boy. Jon and I held each other close. I cannot explain the pain in that moment. I have felt no greater physical or emotional pain in all my life. It was more than I could bear, but I had to bear it. The nurse walked out of the room and Kuyper was gone.

As the nurses moved me to my postpartum room, I could hear the hearty cries of healthy newborns. I prayed in those moments that no mother would ever know this kind of pain again. I prayed for pregnant friends and those who were barely acquaintances. "Lord, let us be the last." A storm hit the city as I entered my room. A fury of rain and thunder rattled the windows. Somehow, the rain seemed to calm my plagued mind and I drifted off into a deep sleep.

The next morning came early, as it always does in hospitals. Waking, I hoped that the previous day's events had all been a bad dream but there I was in a hospital bed. It was real. I walked into the bathroom and was astonished at the sight. My face and eyes were puffy and distorted from all the tears of the previous day, but it was more than that. Just the day before I had looked in the mirror at the me I had always known. Now I looked in the mirror at someone new, someone I did not yet recognize, someone who was in the process of becoming. That new me had years of grief and brokenness ahead of her. But do not lose heart—the years of brokenness are the years God used to rebuild my soul.

A Psalm for Reflection

Psalm 143

Hear my prayer, O LORD;
listen to my plea!
Answer me because you are faithful and righteous.
Don't put your servant on trial,
for no one is innocent before you.
My enemy has chased me.
He has knocked me to the ground
and forces me to live in darkness like those in the grave.
I am losing all hope;
I am paralyzed with fear.
I remember the days of old.
I ponder all your great works
and think about what you have done.
I lift my hands to you in prayer.
I thirst for you as parched land thirsts for rain. Interlude

Come quickly, LORD, and answer me,
for my depression deepens.
Don't turn away from me,
or I will die.
Let me hear of your unfailing love each morning,
for I am trusting you.
Show me where to walk,
for I give myself to you.
Rescue me from my enemies, LORD;
I run to you to hide me.
Teach me to do your will,

for you are my God.
May your gracious Spirit lead me forward on a firm footing.
For the glory of your name, O LORD, preserve my life.
Because of your faithfulness, bring me out of this distress.
In your unfailing love, silence all my enemies
and destroy all my foes,
for I am your servant (NLT).

CHAPTER SIX

When Life is Gripped by Fear

"No one ever told me that grief felt so like fear."

—C.S. Lewis (A Grief Observed)

My mind goes there. Over and over it goes there. I remember as a twelve-year-old waiting up in bed straining to hear the sound of tires contacting the driveway signaling that my dad had made it home. This was pre-everyone had a cellphone. Now I sound old. If someone was not home by the time they said they would be home, you just had to wait. So I would wait—anxiously. Fear gripping my thoughts, "What if he fell asleep while driving and was in an accident? What if he had a heart attack? What if…" and on and on it would go. I still find myself doing this. Somehow after someone you love dies it becomes easier and easier to go down dark mental roads. Deep down you know that the world is no longer as safe as it once seemed.

There are still days that I allow my mind to travel into spirals of fear. I find myself lying in bed. It is late, but instead of sleeping I wait. I wait to hear the sound of the van tires popping on the gravel parking spot signaling that my husband is home. Then I can truly sleep. He has a cell phone, but half the time the battery is dead, especially when he is out late, usually at a *haus krai* (house cry) or a gathering of the tribe that often ends up going well into the night because the meetings usually start late and everyone wants to have their say. I worry as the hours start to tick by.

Fear is a thief. It is a thief of time, and it is a thief of metal peace. It steals joy. It disturbs by taking potential problems of tomorrow and bringing them into today. Stress levels, and even blood pressure levels, can rise over troubles that may or may not even happen. Sleep is lost over problems that might never come to fruition. Once the "what ifs" start, they pick up speed and move rapidly to the worst-case scenario possible. In those dark nights of worrying, I have begun to mentally plan funerals, stress about how I would never be able to handle it all and agonize over thoughts wondering if something terrible happened to my husband should I stay in PNG or go back to the US. Countless stresses that melt away the minute our gray Estima pulls into our little compound. I breathe. A sense of relief washes over me, and I finally drift off to sleep. The phrase "Do not fear" while it does not appear 365 times

> Fear is a thief. It is a thief of time, and it is a thief of mental peace. It steals joy. It disturbs by taking potential problems of tomorrow and bringing them into today.

in Scripture like some popular Internet memes like to claim. It is used over 100 times in the Bible[10], and it is the Bible's most frequent command[11]. A very straightforward, short command that does not need much explanation; and yet so often it is very easy to give into fear and anxiety especially after one has faced tragedy.

When it comes to fear, it is good to dig in and look at the root of what is actually causing your fear. If you are really honest, what deep down are you believing in moments of anxiety? Last year my best friend helped me work through something called a Gospel Tree that her church uses in their discipleship program to help people identify "bad fruit" or sinful behavior in their lives. The goal of the Gospel Tree is to really help a person identify the root of their behavior and not just deal with symptoms of a problem.

I worked through this with my friend originally to help me get to the root of my ongoing struggle with anger; and it revealed that much of my anger is rooted in fear. In my fear I fail to trust. In my fear I try to control my circumstances and the people around me, and when they do not respond how I want them to, I frequently get angry.

As part of the exercise, my friend asked me, "During these fearful times, who are you? What does this fear reveal that you are believing about your identity?"

"In times of fear," I responded, "I believe I am alone, vulnerable, I do not believe that God has the best for me or that He sees me."

"So you feel you need to be in control because you do not think God has the best for you? What does this say about the work God has done?" my friend asked.

"In those times of fear, I am believing that God is distant. I am believing that He does not see or care about my problems, so I need to be the one controlling my circumstances," I responded.

She pushed further, "What do these beliefs about God say about His character?"

"These beliefs say that God is not a personal God and that He is not a caring God. These beliefs say that circumstances are out of His control and that He does not have my best interest at heart."

"Now you have confessed these beliefs that God is not personal. He is not caring, and things are out of His control," my friend wrote back. "Repentance says, 'I don't actually believe that. I know that it is not true. Then ask, 'Who IS God?' 'Who is He really?'"

Writing out the truths I know to be true about God re-centers me. "God is not an impersonal God- He is a personal God who knows me intimately even better than I know myself. He is a caring God who sees me. He is in complete control which means I don't have to be. He *does* have my best interest at heart. How do I know this to be true?"

- **God is a personal God.** I know this because in Ephesians 1:4-6 He says, "In love he predestined us (me, Ruth) for adoption to himself as sons through Jesus Christ, according to the purpose of his will, to the praise of his glorious grace, with which he has blessed us in the Beloved" *parentheses added*. This verse says that I am chosen, longed for, adopted as His child, loved, and through Christ, He has given me grace. So yes, God is very much a personal God who loves me deeply and gives me grace.
- **He is a caring God.** I know this because in 1 Peter 5:7 He says,

"Cast all your anxiety on him because he cares for you" (me, Ruth) (NIV) *parentheses added.*
- ***He sees me.*** I know this because in Genesis 16:13 it says, "'You are the God who sees me,' for she said, 'I have now seen the One who sees me'" (NIV).
- ***He is in control of my life.*** I know this because Philippians 4:5-7 says, "The Lord is near. Do not be anxious about anything, but in every situation, by prayer and petition, with thanksgiving, present your requests to God. And the peace of God, which transcends all understanding will guard your hearts and your minds in Christ Jesus" (NIV).
- ***He has my best interest at heart.*** I know this because Psalm 27:13 says, "I (Ruth) believe that I shall look upon the goodness of the LORD in the land of the living (*He has good things planned for me on this earth not just in heaven, the next life*). Wait for the LORD; be strong, and let your heart take courage; wait for the Lord" *parentheses added.* We wrapped up the exercise with three final questions.
    1. Do you believe all that you wrote?
    2. Because of this belief, what are you experiencing? (Think along the lines of the fruit of the spirit)
    3. What do you believe about who you are in Christ?

"This exercise can be done daily. What is the fruit of my life showing about who God is and what He has done for me? I really like this process," my friend wrote. "I think it helps me put things into perspective and find true repentance rather than just trying to change my fruit via behavioral modification."

It is so critical to get to that root, that sin issue, especially when it comes to fear. What lies have we allowed ourselves to believe? What wrong ideas about God are we entertaining in our minds when we allow anxiety to control? Are you allowing circumstances to dictate your feelings or are you standing in the unchanging promises found in God's word? 2 Timothy:1:7 Says, "For God has not given us a spirit of fear and timidity, but of power, love and self discipline" (NLT). Replace the fears that try to threaten your thought life with these three things—**rest** in the knowledge that the power of God dwells inside of you, **choose** love over fear and **practice** disciplining your thoughts.

Are you afraid that God does not have your best interest at heart? Are you afraid of again losing someone that you love? I fear loss. I fear pain because I have been there, and it hurts deeply. If I am completely honest I struggle with always truly trusting that God has my best interest at heart, so I often resist resting in His perfect peace.

It is interesting to note how so often responses to grief are intertwined with fear just like they were with how Job's friends responded insensitively to him. Fear can sadly even lead people to blame someone who has recently lost a loved one trying to find fault, in a bizarre way, because it gives a false sense of protection to the person who is afraid of something similar happening to them. This is often so subconscious, but it happens. Three teens were recently killed in a car crash near where my parents live. Most people's comments I read on social media were messages of loving condolence, sadly there were also comments of, "Why were those teens out driving at that hour?" as if driving past midnight means they deserved to die. This tendency to blame heaps pain upon pain and reflects the fear of the one commenting.

With social media and strangers weighing in where they really have no sense of the bigger picture, off handed comments like this can be so hurtful. The last thing someone grieving needs is blame and judgment. Of course, hindsight is 20/20. Don't we all wish at times that we could go back in time and do something differently? But, reality is that we cannot and neither can the person who lost their loved one.

"There is such a pervasive weirdness in our culture around grief and death. We judge, and we blame, dissect, and minimize," writes Megan Devine reflecting on the freak drowning accident that took her partner's life. She shares that the one news story she read covering the accident blamed her partner for his death because he wasn't wearing a life jacket and some comments from people, who she had never met, went as far as calling both her and her partner stupid.

"Especially when the loss is unusual, violent, or accidental, the backlash of blame is intense," Devine writes. "We immediately point out what someone else did wrong… It soothes our brain, in some ways to believe that through our own good sense, we, and all we love can be safe…Seeing someone in pain touches off a reaction in us, and that reaction makes us very uncomfortable. Faced with this visceral knowledge that we, too could be in a similar situation, we shut down our empathy centers. We deny our connection. We shift into judgment and blame. How quick we are to demoralize rather than empathize."[12]

Why is there this tendency? It is rooted completely in fear—

deflecting, blaming and judging instead of entering into a complicated situation in order to comfort. "Why were they out walking alone? Why was the medicine cabinet left unlocked? Why were they not wearing a seatbelt? Why was their child not vaccinated? Why did they not take him to the hospital sooner...? Let us commit to stopping this practice of letting subconscious fears taint our responses to grief. We live in an imperfect broken, broken world where tragic things can happen to anyone in spite of our best precautions. It is a scary reality. Instead of blaming, consciously choose to once again weep with those who weep regardless of the complicated circumstances surrounding a death.

It is important to learn how to control fear instead of letting fear control us. Whether that be in how we respond to other people's tragedy or how we face the fear of what could happen in our own lives. Fear is a choice just as trust is a choice. The idea of taking thoughts captive is a practice that I have not often engaged with. It is easy to see thoughts as passive and let them spiral and skip around the mind as they wish. But what you think affects how you live life, so this is a harmful approach. As Christians, we cannot simply allow our thoughts to roam. We must choose, and choose carefully, what we allow our minds to mull over. My son's memory verse this week is Philippians 4:8—"Whatever is true, whatever is noble, whatever is right, whatever is pure, whatever is lovely, whatever is admirable—if anything is excellent or praiseworthy—think about such things." (NIV)

What a mental weight can be lifted if we simply choose to follow this practice. Try it this week. If fear or anxiety is a tendency in your life, choose to dwell on God's goodness instead. Find a verse and read it every time anxious thoughts try to creep into your mind. For me it is often 1 John 4:18 "There is no fear in love, but perfect love casts out fear." This verse actually calmed my heart when it came to giving birth to my first-born. You can ask my family and friends, for the longest time I said I would rather adopt than go through labor. As a redhead with a very low pain tolerance, I had always been paralyzed by the thought of the physical pain of labor, so when I was faced with giving birth in a country and at a hospital with no option for an epidural I struggled. But, by choosing love over fear (and after a lot of reading up on natural birth) I was able to find strength in 1 John 4:18 and face one of my greatest fears which has of course led to one of the greatest blessings in my life—my children.

There is no need to allow fear to grip your life because God's love for you is perfect. Choose, every day, to dwell in love over dwelling in fear. Fear can lead to stress that can physically and mentally damage your body. When fear starts to creep, actively fight. One piece of practical advice that has helped me so much is from the book *Having a Mary Heart in a Martha World*. "Here's what I did," Joanna Weaver writes. "Instead of mentally obsessing about my problems, I began consciously turning my worry into prayer. Instead of worrying, 'What if my husband has a wreck while he's on the road,' I'd pray, 'Dear Jesus, be with John as he drives today...' That may sound trite and overly simplistic, but something in this tiny act broke the bondage. Rather than nursing and rehearsing my concerns, I began giving them over to the Lord. And gradually as I did, I found that chronic anxiety had lost its grip on me. You see, fretting magnifies the *problem*, but prayer magnifies *God*."[13]

Why pray? Prayer can actually help a situation improve. Fear and stress make it worse. So, when my husband is out late and his phone goes to voicemail, instead of jumping on the worry train I can choose to stop—acknowledge the fear and instead say a prayer for God to give my husband protection as he drives home. I do this with my kids as well. If I am not physically with them and start to feel the anxiety of the "what ifs," I take a minute to pray for them knowing that I can choose to continue to think about the bad things that could be happening; or I can choose to remember all the times that God has protected my family and find mental rest in that.

Borrowing problems that have not yet happened is walking down a road you were never asked to walk down. God is not going to give you the grace and strength to face nonexistent problems. He will only give the grace and strength needed to walk though actual trials. People expressed this to my parents after my sister died when they said things like "I don't know how I would survive losing a child." Now, as a parent, I think this myself. But, the people who said this to my parents were not asked, at that point in their life, to face the trial of losing a child. So no, of course, they could not comprehend it. My parents, I am sure, could not comprehend how to face it either before God met them at the exact time of their need and gave them the daily comfort they needed to make it through each hard day.

Fear is a thief, but you can put mental fences up in your mind to make it harder for the thief to attack. Be bold—choose to take the day, the problems, and the trials as they come (but not before).

Give mental energy to actual issues not the "what ifs" and worries of the future. I am preaching to myself now, but at the same time I am so thankful for the perfect peace that can be found in the one who gives peace that passes all understanding.

> "The Lord is my light and my salvation—whom shall I fear? The Lord is the stronghold of my life—of whom shall I be afraid?"
> —Psalm 27:1 (NIV)

The Strong One

By Stephanie Clarke

"MRS. BLOOMFIELD?" the school secretary chimed in over the loudspeaker.

"Yes?"

"Please send Stephanie Prater to the office. She will be leaving."

I already had my backpack ready. I had been anticipating the call since arriving at school that morning. The plan was that my aunt would pick me and my siblings up at our respective schools and take us to meet our mom at the hospital where our dad was getting a check-up.

He had been diagnosed with a very rare lung disease called pulmonary alveolar proteinosis when I was six years old. The doctors told us that there was no cure but that treatment could be done to elongate his life. The only problem was that, in the late 80s, only a few hospitals did the specific treatment; and my Dad was adamant he was not going to uproot his family and move us some four states away.

So for five years, I watched him. I watched him struggle as his breathing gradually became more labored. I watched his color slowly diminish as the abscesses in his lungs spread to his brain. I watched the home health nurse give him IV fluids, eventually showing us how to administer them through the tube in his chest.

And I intently watched the rise and fall of his every respiration while lying there in his arms the night before his check-up, his eyes glued to his beloved *Three Stooges* on the television.

I can still faintly hear his cough-interrupted laughter. I can still remember his fingers running through his little girl's hair. Though his arms had weakened significantly to what they once were, I still felt so safe in that moment. So safe, I didn't want the morning to come.

But it did. My mom, now running on pure adrenaline, made sure we were all in the car, dropped us off at our schools that morning; and then she and my dad made the two hour journey to the hospital in Lexington.

I remember sitting in science class that day, cognizant of the fact that my dad's appointment was around the very same hour. My desk was next to the wall of windows that were usually cheery with light. But after taking attendance, the teacher pulled the blinds to the windows and turned on a film for us to watch. I don't remember the topic the film was discussing that day. I don't even recall there being anyone else in the room. All I remember was that feeling of anxiety that came over me that hour.

It felt like time had stopped. Like the inertia of the moment was telling my gut that something just wasn't right. Tears started to stream down my face uncontrollably. The darkness felt smothering. I needed light. Someone needed to raise the blinds. Scanning the room, my science teacher stopped at my desk and approached me.

"Stephanie, are you alright?"

I couldn't respond with words. All I could do was lift my head, look into his eyes, and shake my head to gesture "no."

He gently helped me out of my chair and took me outside in the hallway.

"What's wrong?"

"It's him. Something is wrong my dad. Can you tell me what's wrong with my dad?"

He went next door to Mrs. Bloomfield and together they did their best to wipe my tears and reassure me. I didn't want to be there. I wanted to be with the man whose arms made me feel safe. The man whose tomato soup and grilled cheese would have put the local diner's to shame. I wanted to be with the man who would stand on that first base line coaching his little league team all the while keeping a mindful eye on me. I wanted to be with him.

Insistent that I didn't want to go back into that dark room, Mrs. Bloomfield escorted me back to her empty room. It was her planning period, but empty resembled everything that I felt at that moment. I sat at my desk, trying to compose myself. She would lift her head from her writing every now and then to just check on me, but words fell short for both of us. Maybe she knew something too.

Minutes passed and the bell rang. My classmates joined me in her room for our next class. Numb to it all, I just sat there watching the second-hand on the clock tick. Seconds turned into minutes. Minutes slowly turned into hours. And finally, I heard the call:

"Mrs. Bloomfield?"

"Yes?"

"Please send Stephanie Prater to the office. She will be leaving."

I took my backpack from my chair and made my way up the aisle. I looked her in the eye and remember her murmuring, "Take all the time that you need." I nodded my head and walked out the door. Those words would replay in my mind taking that long walk down the sixth grade hallway. I turned the corner to the office, saw my aunt, and breathed a sigh of relief. With all the premonitions I'd had that morning, I whispered a prayer that it would be her face that I'd see and not my mom's. I knew that if I saw my mom's face he was gone.

She signed me out, held my hand and led me out of the school building. The heavy metal door latched behind us, and l lifted my head.

"What's she doing here, Aunt Gretchen?"

There was silence as my aunt looked toward the car. Inside sat my mom staring out the window at me.

"What's she doing here?" I asked again.

"Come on, Stephie. Let's go and pick up your brother and sister and head home."

Home? Head home? Tentatively, I walked down those steps, reluctantly opened the car door, soberly sat in the back seat, and deliberately stared out the window. I couldn't face my mom. Because to face her meant that her eyes would reveal the truth–and my heart wasn't quite ready to accept what my mind already knew.

My daddy was gone. He was only 37.

Two days later, I stood at his casket, looking at his chest. I waited. I waited for the rise and fall of a respiration. I inched closer, bravely put my hand on his chest, and waited.

"Breathe, Daddy. Breathe." I pleaded.

But he didn't. He couldn't. I looked up at his face, worn from illness, stilled by death.

Tiptoeing, I tearfully leaned over, kissed his cold cheek, and whispered in his ear, "I love you, Daddy."

As people started streaming into the visitation, I couldn't stay there. I needed some fresh air. So I made my way outside to the funeral's front porch and sat on the bench there. A few moments later, a great aunt that I'd not seen in years joined me. She sat down next to me, took my hand in hers, offered her condolences and then said, "You know, Stephanie, you have to be the strong one for your mom and siblings."

Me? Beyond the fact that I had just lost the only man I'd ever loved, I was eleven! ELEVEN! And I, the youngest of the family, am supposed to be the strong one?

I'm sure she had good intentions, or maybe she just didn't know what to say, but I believed her. For years I bore that burden—of being the strong one—and repressed grieving my Dad. Inside my heart remained broken, but outside I made sure that at least my resolve looked strong. I learned to smile bravely despite the pain, to laugh willfully despite the sorrow, to love cautiously despite the loss.

And as the saying goes, life went on. My mom remarried, and we all went through the growing pains of building a stepfamily. I graduated at the top of my high school class like I promised my daddy I'd do. I landed a good job after college, and a couple years later, wedded my Bajan husband and joined him in the ministry in his native island.

Things were far from perfect, but they were good.

Good enough that I never saw it coming.

The day started as normal. I dropped our 10-month-old daughter off at her grandmother's and our three-year-old son off at his preschool. Then I went to the office. I remember sitting at my desk that morning and my heart began to rapidly palpitate. It felt as though needles were going through a million different points in my skin, and I couldn't breathe. Being well-versed in displaying a strong resolve, I got up, went outside, called my husband and told him that if anything happened to me to make sure that he told the kids that I loved them and to be sure that he took them to see my family. From the way I was feeling, I literally thought I was going to die– die young, just like my dad.

I asked my co-worker to drive me to the urgent care clinic. After they did an EKG on my heart, along with some other tests, to rule out a heart attack, the doctor came in, handed me a paper that read "generalized anxiety disorder" and referred me to a psychiatrist.

I guess unresolved grief has a way of surfacing after all– even some two decades later. Thankfully, in His omniscience, God had already placed a very compassionate mentor in my life. She recognized that the 30-minute sessions with the psychiatrist were not helping to get to the root of the problem. As the attacks continued to persist, the next one always worse than the last. So, she instinctively booked me at a retreat center where I would go through a week of intensive Christian counseling sessions with the clinical psychologist on staff.

It was there that healing began. It was there that, at the age of 33, I was finally given permission to mourn– permission to not only mourn the loss of his life and of time, but permission to let go of the burden of responsibility that I had carried all those years to be "the strong one" and the subsequent guilt and fear that I was not doing it well. Because, as it turns out, there is The Strong One whose strength is perfect and who's Word declares that He is near to the brokenhearted. So it IS okay to be broken.

As it turns out, there is The Strong One who Himself wept and whose Word assures us that there IS a time for everything and a season for every activity under the heavens – even to mourn. It IS okay to express deep sorrow.

The Strong One invites us to come, to rest, to let Him share in our burden of grief. So it IS okay to walk through that process, for we do not walk alone. I don't have to be the strong one – and neither do you, friend. Jesus already is.

A Psalm for Reflection

Psalm 34

I will praise the LORD at all times.
I will constantly speak his praises.
I will boast only in the LORD;
let all who are helpless take heart.
Come, let us tell of the LORD's greatness
let us exalt his name together.

I prayed to the LORD, and he answered me.
He freed me from all my fears.
Those who look to him for help will be radiant with joy;
no shadow of shame will darken their faces.
In my desperation I prayed, and the Lord listened;
he saved me from all my troubles.
For the angel of the LORD is a guard;
he surrounds and defends all who fear him.

Taste and see that the LORD is good.
Oh, the joys of those who take refuge in him!
Fear the LORD, you his godly people,
for those who fear him will have all they need.
Even strong young lions sometimes go hungry,
but those who trust in the LORD will lack no good thing.

Come, my children, and listen to me,
and I will teach you to fear the LORD.
Does anyone want to live a life
that is long and prosperous?

*Then keep your tongue from speaking evil
and your lips from telling lies!
Turn away from evil and do good.
Search for peace, and work to maintain it.*

*The eyes of the LORD watch over those who do right;
his ears are open to their cries for help.
But the Lord turns his face against those who do evil;
he will erase their memory from the earth.
The Lord hears his people when they call to him for help
He rescues them from all their troubles.
The LORD is close to the brokenhearted;
he rescues those whose spirits are crushed.*

*The righteous person faces many troubles,
but the LORD comes to the rescue each time.
For the LORD protects the bones of the righteous
not one of them is broken!*

*Calamity will surely destroy the wicked,
and those who hate the righteous will be punished.
But the LORD will redeem those who serve him.
No one who takes refuge in him will be condemned. (NLT)*

CHAPTER SEVEN

Is God Good to Me?

> *"Other people are going to find healing in your wounds. Your greatest messages and your most effective ministry will come out of your deepest hurts."*
>
> —Rick Warren (The Purpose Driven Life)

"I know God is good, but what I struggle with at times is, the idea that He is good to me." As someone who has faced just about every trial possible, Vaneetha Rendall Risner (author of *The Scars that Have Shaped Me*), is no stranger to suffering which has understandably led her to ask that inevitable question—is a God who allows so much suffering good? Vaneetha contracted polio as a baby and was left paralyzed when her polio was mistreated. She spent years in and out of hospitals seeking treatment and was bullied due to the physical challenges she faced. As an adult, life did not get easier. She suffered multiple miscarriages and then tragically lost her infant son who was born with a heart condition and later died when a doctor made a fatal mistake. Her husband abandoned her for another woman leaving her to raise two daughters on her own. It is hard to even begin to comprehend the pain Vaneetha has faced during her life. No wonder she has asked herself the question, "Is God good to me?"[14]

It is not a new question. How can any of this be good? Sure we quote Romans 8:28 "And we know that for those who love God all things work together for good, for those who are called according to His purpose." But, do we really believe it? Can we really see the big picture that pain can bring good?

As I type, Covid-19 seems to be affecting every corner of the earth. How is that good? My sister lost her job due to Covid cut backs. She and her family had to move because they could no longer afford rent in the area where they had been living. My husband's long time friend just messaged from London that he has tested positive for the virus and was admitted to the hospital due to blood clots in both of his lungs.[15] There have already been two funerals this month at our church: a young mom who gave birth to a baby just three weeks ago and another friend who met a guy online, and after moving in with him, ended up contracting a disease that took her life not long after it took his.

Why doesn't God just stop all of the tragedy? He is all-powerful right? Like the mystery of the trinity, the challenge of explaining how an all powerful and all loving God can allow so much brokenness in the world is not easy. Many excellent books like Philip Yancey's *Where is God When It Hurts?* and *When God Weeps* by Joni Eareckson Tada's and Steve Estes (just to scratch the surface of available resources) spend pages and pages looking much more in-depth at this important question; so this chapter will just touch the proverbial surface. But, I will say that the answer is not as simple as we often try to make it. I have a dear friend whose daughter passed away from a brain tumor. When her daughter was sick and someone would tell her "God is in control," she would respond, "What if my daughter dies?" Not an easy question to answer. A few years ago my niece's toddler son nearly drowned. We waited anxiously for news that he was ok. When I got the message that he was not only going to make it, but that his brain was not negatively affected, and he was set to return home soon, I shot back the response, "God is good. To which my niece replied, "Yes, He is." Then I caught myself. Would I have been so quick to use that phrase if the outcome had been different? It is so easy to equate God being good with getting the answer that we desperately, desperately desire. What about when the child dies, or when the cancer that was in remission returns? What about the man who was senselessly murdered? Is God still good? Is He still in control?

How could a loving God who is in complete control allow the death of my dear friend's daughter? Part of the human brain wants to scream, "No! an all loving God could never allow it!" So the all-powerfulness of God is sacrificed in favor of Him being all-loving. This is the conclusion that Rabbi Harold Kushner comes to in his bestselling book *When Bad Things Happen to Good People*. After the tragic loss of His young son, Kushner concludes that God is, in fact, not fully in control but that He is all loving.[16] But, does the Bible support this conclusion or are verses and circumstances being hammered into a tiny box that they were never meant to fit into?

The phrase that helped Joni Eareckson Tada through her struggle of being paralyzed from the neck down during a diving accident reflects a different perspective. "Sometimes God allows what He hates to accomplish what He loves."[17] There are times that God chooses to allow pain. There are times when pain comes as a natural part of living in a world tainted by sin and disease. Like Joseph's response to his brothers "you meant evil against me, but God meant it for good" (Genesis 50:20). God has a way of working in the midst of even the deepest hurts. He sees the big picture. We see the pain. Like the refiner's fire, pain can also cleanse the heart and often grows us even closer to our creator. As C.S. Lewis so wisely puts it, "Pain insists upon being attended to. God whispers to us in our pleasures, speaks in our conscience, but shouts in our pains. It is his megaphone to rouse a deaf world."[18]

We are comfortable. We are deaf, but then pain hits and we cannot ignore the struggle any longer, a struggle which often leads us into a closer relationship with the Father if we choose to allow it to do so.

I have found the idea of God being nearest in times of pain to be so true in my own life. Of course, I would have rather my twin sister had not died, especially so young; but I will say I have never felt God's presence as strongly as I did as an eight year old during that immense time of pain. God was there. He used that time of deep pain to grow me. I became a more compassionate and empathetic person because of the loss that happened so early in my life. Could God have stopped her death? Yes, and yet she is now in a place with no more sickness and pain. Many of us, left on earth, took a step closer to heaven because of the experience of losing Allison.

God never told Job why he went through all the pain and grief that he experienced, instead He spoke through the storm reminding Job that He sends the rain and creates the snow. Everything is under His control and dominion. Job then realigned his thinking. He did not go away with a *why* answered but with a *who*. He saw clearly who was in control, an all-knowing, all-powerful God—a God whose thoughts and ways are higher than the thoughts and ways of His creation. With this knowledge, Job again found peace. As readers, we see a clear picture. Job's life became a lasting reminder to the enemy that there was a righteous man on earth who, in spite of every hardship thrown at him, maintained his righteousness; but Job was never told any of this. He was again restored to a life of ease and blessing, but he was never given the reason for why all the tragedy happened.

Sometimes God does allow us to see how our loss is heaven's gain- how *He* receives glory when we are asked to walk a difficult road. And then, God the Father, also endured the loss of a son in order to bring about the salvation of humanity. He allowed His beloved son to die a painful death on the cross. That sting of death was very real, and yet that death opened the way for broken sinners to find life eternal. Without the death of an innocent Savior this never would have been possible.

I love the line in the song "Seasons" by Hillsong that talks about how a seed can be buried, even in the snow, and yet it is waiting for its time of growth.[19] One of the great mysteries of the agricultural world is that the death of the seed can actually bring about new life. How mind-boggling is that. We see the dark, the death, the decay; but God's vision shows the life and growth that will come in abundance when the next season comes.

I carried an orange and blue pocket sized Bible in college. The cover has just about worn off, but my husband still keeps it. It was sitting at his desk the other day, so I used it when looking up a reference. On an empty back page of the Bible, I saw notes scribbled from a sermon Pastor Scott Ziegler preached on suffering. I must have been out of paper that particular Sunday. I do not normally take notes directly in my Bible, but I am glad that I did that week because the words are still such a good reminder of some of the reasons that a loving God allows suffering. My scribbled notes serve as a reminder that the purpose of suffering is:

- For our learning
- For our improvement
- For God's glory
- For others benefit

So be faithful even to the point of death. Revelations 2:10[20]

When suffering and death feel like too much, work on zooming out your perspective. It is easy to see a small picture and focus only on the pain. God sees the bigger picture and the good that can come even from the deepest hurt. Maybe in our lifetime we will be allowed to see some of the good that came from the pain, or maybe (like with Job) it will not be until heaven that we understand the bigger picture more clearly. With my sister's death, I know that it changed me. I would not be writing this book for one thing if I had not gone through the experience that I did. Her death also opened up many doors in the Congolese community where my parents were serving as missionaries because it helped my parents relate and minister better to the many families in the community who had also lost loved ones.

One of my parents' supporting churches started a summer camp scholarship in memory of my sister that helped provide a yearly scholarship for many different kids (including me for two summers) to attend summer camp. It was a simple gesture, in a way, but a special one. I know the years that I was able to go to camp on that scholarship grew me as I am sure it grew and changed the many other children who also received a scholarship in my sister's memory.

One day, in a Chicago hospital, my parents got to hear another positive that came from Allison's death. They were with friends whose young daughter was dying after years of fighting aggressive liver disease. While chatting with another family, who was at the hospital for a completely different reason, my mom shared about why they were there doing what they could to support and comfort their friends since she and my dad had also walked the road of facing the loss of a child.

"Wait," the lady stopped her, "Are you Allison's mom?" Her daughter had attended an AWANA program at one of the churches that supported our family. After Allison had passed away, the church had shared the story with the AWANA group and one of the young girls (who was just a few years older than Allison) heard the story and decided to become a missionary. The girl's mom told my mom that her daughter would be going on her first mission trip to South America that summer. A young life touched by a story of pain. Because of that touch, her life took an entirely different bend then it would have otherwise.

There is good. Sometimes we get to hear those stories of how God used the pain we went through to bring good in an entirely different realm. Sometimes they happen without us ever knowing it, but God knows. He sees, and He orchestrates things that are beyond our individual worlds to bring about a greater good.

I think about the five young missionaries whose story is told in the book, *Through the Gates of Splendor*. Five lives tragically lost when missionaries attempted to befriend the Auca tribe in South America, yet think about how many others had their hearts turned towards missions because they heard this story of sacrifice. God again worked to bring about good from painful circumstances.

At the beginning of the chapter, I referenced Romans 8:28 a verse that is commonly quoted to those going through grief almost to the point that some people do not find it to be a comfort. They see it instead as trying to stretch a tiny Band-Aid on a gaping wound. In Hannah Anderson's book, *All That's Good: Recovering the Lost Art of Discernment*, she points out that Romans 8:28 is often taken out of context. "We often quote Romans 8:28 to each other in times of crisis: 'We know that all things work together for the good of those who love God, who are called according to his purpose.' What we mean is something like, 'Every cloud has a silver lining.' Or 'You can't have a rainbow without a little rain.' But when you continue reading in verse 29, you discover that God means something else entirely. 'For those he foreknew he also predestined to be conformed to the image of his Son.' In other words, God's idea of what is good for us is often different from our idea of what would be good for us. God intends to make us holy, and He will use whatever it takes to reach that good—including—suffering."[21] So what is the good that God is at work doing? It is the very specific work of conforming us to the image of His Son. Just as Christ suffered, our suffering makes us more like Christ. That is the good that comes from suffering as painful as it might be.

It is easy to bristle against the idea that God uses suffering for our good. There is a strange, unspoken idea in modern Christianity that if we follow God and live a good Christian life, we will somehow be immune to suffering (or at least our suffering will be minimal). Our children will be healthy, marriages happy and life overall free from the problems that pledge the rest of humanity—a sort of earthly reward for being moral. Scripture does not support this idea. In fact, it says the opposite—Matthew 5:45 says, "For he makes his sun rise on the evil and on the good, and sends rain on the just and the unjust." These subtle false teachings of "bad things should not happen to good people," have subconsciously wound themselves into the minds of too many believers. They are poison because they can leave a Christian devastated when suffering does touch their lives, leaving them asking, "What did I do wrong?" "Is God really good?" "Why is this happening to me?" Yet, Christ has told us that suffering *will* happen. "In this world you will have trouble" (John 16:33 NIV) clearly states. It is not necessarily someone's fault when something bad happens. Just like in the story of the man born blind in John 9:1-12, when the disciples ask Jesus whose fault was it that this man was born blind, was it the fault of the parents or the man? Jesus corrects their theology by answering. It was not the result of this man's sin or his parents' sin that he was born blind. There was a *purpose*. God allowed the blindness so that He would eventually be glorified through the man's suffering. Jesus then proceeds to heal the blind man's eyes and, in doing so, brought glory to his

Father.

There is a bigger picture, a larger story—something so much greater than ourselves. We need to lift our heads up from our own carefully crafted plans so that we can see how the plan we have been asked to walk through is being used for God's glory. If we begin to do that, we will often find the good that is there. Is the suffering pleasant? Of course not, so we should not minimize that; but we should also not miss the growth and lessons that need to be learned because we are too focused on the pain to see a greater plan—maybe a different plan from the one that we had, but a plan for good.

One of the evangelists at our church here in Papua New Guinea loves to tell the story of a man who would come home every day with a bag of groceries and his wife would call out, "God is good." To which he would respond, "All the time" and hand her the groceries.

One day the man came home without his usual bag of food and when his wife called out "God is good." The empty-handed man shook his head and responded, "Not this time." We don't often admit it, but sadly this can be how we view God. When things are going well, "God is

> There is a bigger picture, a larger story—something so much greater than ourselves. We need to lift our heads up from our own carefully crafted plans so that we can see how the plan we have been asked to walk through is being used for God's glory.

good." When suffering hits, "Why God are you not being good to me?"

Do we see God's goodness as conditional? Does it mean always having healthy children? Does it mean living a full life with your partner? Does it mean houses of feasting but not houses of mourning? We are so quick to recite wedding vows of, "In sickness and in health, for richer or for poorer for better or worse." But, the high divorce rate shows that these vows are often not followed through. Too many times when life no longer feels good, when things get hard, there is the temptation to simply check out. There are couples who have ended their marriage after a child was born with a disability. Sometimes the death of a loved one is also followed by divorce adding pain upon pain. When it all feels like too much, it is tempting to cut out what does not seem to be working. Sometimes we do this to God as well. Grief hits—a death, a disaster and thoughts come that, "Maybe this just is not working any more. Maybe God is not really good." The focus is on temporary happiness and feelings. Our focus needs to be *refocused* on trusting that God truly does have our good in mind just as His word promises.

Before my husband and I got married, whenever I had the chance, I would ask inter-cultural couples for any advice they were willing to share. I noticed my husband (fiancé at the time) loved to ask older couples to share their marriage wisdom. I loved the advice that my grandma gave him. "We come from a generation where if something is broken you fix it, you don't throw it out." In other words, don't end a marriage just because it gets hard. When you have problems, do what you can to fix them. Struggle through it, but struggle through it together and come out stronger on the other end. This is actually good advice for much of life. Things in this sin-tainted world are broken, so instead of throwing out faith when things get hard, struggle through and come out with a stronger faith. Suffering often shapes the sufferer into a more compassionate, more mature, more understanding person who is better able to relate to the broken world around them.

I love the perspective that Shadrach, Meshach, and Abednego had when threatened with death because they refused to bow before King Nebuchadnezzar's statue. "If we are thrown into the blazing furnace, the God we serve is able to deliver us from it, and he will deliver us from your Majesty's hand. But even if he does not, we want you to know we will not serve your gods or worship the image of gold you have set up." Daniel 3:17-18 (NIV) The three friend's devotion was not conditional. In the midst of a literal fiery trial they committed to trusting God, who they knew had the power to save them, and yet they were determined to stay true to their all powerful God even if He did not choose to rescue them from suffering. God is all-powerful, and He is still good to His children even when trials come.

Find the good in the hard. Trust the process; do not let the process consume you. Learn the lessons that God has to teach and find hope in the truth that while suffering and pain are very real and hard, good can be found even in the most difficult of circumstances and experiences. Hold tightly to the hope—a hope that allows us to grieve in light of the bigger narrative of eternity, a hope that reminds us that we are living one chapter at a time knowing that in the final scene death is conquered forever—

finished—crushed—banished from the sweet glory of a pain free heaven.

> "But as for me, it is good to be near God. I have made the sovereign LORD My refuge: I will tell of all your deeds." —Psalms 73:26 (NIV)

He Gives and Takes Away

By Pastor Donald Erickson

I STILL REMEMBER the afternoon we found out our daughter, Kara, had been diagnosed with Type-1 Juvenile Diabetes. Kara hadn't been feeling well and my wife, Claudia, had just returned from taking her to see our pediatrician. The prognosis wasn't good. Kara's glucose levels were high, and everything pointed to what would become a lifelong chronic disease without a cure. We needed to pack for the long ride into Chicago to Children's Memorial Hospital; but all we wanted to do was stand in the kitchen, hug each other and cry.

That September day would be the first of many trips to hospitals and doctors' offices. Over the next fifteen years, we would find ourselves searching for the right set of doctors and the right hospital to address the specific needs of our daughter. We would also discover that in order to avoid having hospital doctors treat Kara like every other diabetic, we had to become her personal advocate. There were times when the stress of seeing our daughter's health mismanaged took its toll on us as her parents just as it did on her.

In the early stages of Kara's illness, we found ourselves in "medical school," learning as much as we could about this life altering disease. We found ourselves learning about glucose levels, ketoacidosis, insulin resistance and test strips among other things. We had hands-on training in using a glucometer, filling syringes and administering insulin shots. While we readily admit we never chose to sign up for such duty, we quickly realized that if we were going to walk this journey with our daughter, we had no choice.

While we were learning what it meant to walk alongside a daughter with a serious disease, we were also learning what it meant to have God walking alongside us as we navigated these uncharted waters. I can't begin to tell you how many different times in so many different places we found ourselves needing to find the right hospital at the right time to care for Kara, when her body would suddenly decide to shut down. It could be a family vacation in Florida, a business trip in Kentucky, or a getaway weekend with a friend in Michigan, it didn't really matter. All of a sudden, Kara's blood sugars would skyrocket, and her internal organs would begin to go haywire and quickly we needed to find the best available care. And time and again, God reaffirmed that we were at the right hospital and the right doctors were attending to her needs.

Two months after Claudia and I were married, God called me into ministry. Surprise! Not that I have ever regretted that call. In fact, I can't imagine doing anything else. But, quite frankly, ministry and a seriously ill child can make for a very stressful life. But, for whatever reason, both my wife and I felt very strongly that we were exactly where God wanted us to be and that part of His calling on our lives included parenting four very precious children, one of whom had some very challenging medical needs.

Serving as a pastor is not the most lucrative vocation, yet throughout our lives we have seen God bless us over and over again, far beyond anything we ever deserved and that included incredible medical care and the financial resources to pay for it. We learned to be grateful to God for all the blessings of life because at a moment's notice, we could find ourselves crying out to Him for help in the uncertain times.

As Kara moved into her early teen years, her health issues became more complicated which led to more doctor appointments and more hospitalizations. By her early twenties, her body continued to deteriorate. Her entire body began to suffer ongoing aches and pain. One of the side effects of the disease is neuropathy, which is the damage caused to one or more of the nerves in the body. In Kara's case, the nerves in her joints were affected and she was eventually diagnosed with total body pain. Kara understood the misery of Job when he writes, "The night racks my bones and the pain that gnaws me takes no rest" (Job 30:17). Kara's doctors prescribed various drugs in an attempt to help her manage the pain, but nothing took away the pain. From time to time, Kara would tell us, "I don't understand why God is allowing this, but I need to trust Him." In her own way I think she was reflecting the words of the Apostle Paul in 2 Corinthians 12:10 "For when I am weak, then I am strong."

So, what does a young lady, whose body is racked with pain, do following graduation from high school? Go to massage therapy school, of course! While I know exactly why she chose this vocation, I don't know how she managed to complete her course work and get her certification. But she did!

Kara's career as a massage therapist didn't last very long. While she was very good at what she did, the rigors of what she was required to do took its toll on her body, and over the course of a couple of years she realized she needed to fold up her table and put it away in storage. Several years later, when our church developed a medical outreach ministry to our community, her massage table became a very useful piece of equipment for examining patients.

Over the years following Kara's diagnosis, diabetic research advanced significantly. Diagnostic equipment was perfected. Insulin pump technology improved to where she no longer had to give herself shots three or four times a day. Our hope was that, in time, medical research would discover a cure for this wretched disease. While we never saw a cure, we were encouraged by the reports we were hearing concerning stem cell research and pancreas transplants. Our hope was that Kara might be a candidate for either the transplantation of insulin producing islets or a pancreas transplant.

As I use the word hope, I am reminded that at a human level, hope is wishing for something that may or may not actually happen. We did a lot of that. When dealing with the reality of a life-threatening disease, one's life from day to day can be filled with the ups and downs of human hope. One day excited about the possibilities and the next day disappointed with the unfulfilled expectations. But there is another level to our hope that comes when we put our faith and trust in Jesus Christ. That hope is not about wishful thinking but rather about a trust in the certainty of the future. Romans, Chapter 5 talks about this hope in the context of suffering. "Through him we have also obtained access by faith into this grace in which we stand, and we rejoice in hope of the glory of God. Not only that, but we rejoice in our sufferings, knowing that suffering produces endurance, and endurance produces character, and character produces hope, and hope does not put us to shame, because God's love has been poured into our hearts through the Holy Spirit who has been given to us" (Romans 5:2-5). While our human hope kept us looking for solutions for Kara's illness, our hope in Jesus Christ kept our faith firmly planted on what was eternal.

Kara eventually received a pancreas transplant, which is a whole other story. In actuality, she traded all the medical prescriptions to treat her diabetes for another set of medical prescriptions to keep her body from rejecting her new pancreas. That lasted for about 18 months, when sadly, her body won, and her new pancreas lost. With her body rejecting the new pancreas, we were back to treating the diabetes.

With the return to the life of a diabetic, the next year was both disappointing and filled with more doctors and hospital visits. In September 2004, Kara's blood sugars began to skyrocket, and her body once again was going into ketoacidosis with her organs shutting down. As she had done so many other times before, my wife drove our daughter the fifty some miles to the hospital that had so wonderfully cared for her before. The medical staff was able to get her stabilized and after almost a week of treatment, Kara was able to come home.

The day Kara came home from the hospital, her twin sisters were in the audience at the Oprah Winfrey show when Oprah gave away brand new Pontiac G6 cars to everyone attending that show.

While our daughters had permission to tell their immediate family the incredible news, we were all sworn to secrecy until after the show aired on TV the following Monday morning.

Monday morning, we all watched the Oprah show and were beyond excited for our daughters. Since our house was right across the street from the church I was pastoring, I headed back to my office to study. But about an hour later, my wife called me to tell me that Kara wasn't doing well and that I needed to come home. It didn't take long after I got there to realize that something was seriously wrong and we weren't going to be able to drive Kara to the hospital as we had done so many times before. We called the paramedics, who arrived within minutes. After an assessment of the situation, it was apparent that Kara needed to be transported to the nearest hospital. I did something I had never done before, I rode in the back of the ambulance with my daughter. Little did I realize it would be the last trip to the hospital I would ever take with her.

When we got to the hospital, they took her immediately into emergency and after a series of tests, we were informed that our daughter had suffered a heart attack. After years of dealing with high glucose levels, neuropathy, temporary loss of vision and a failed transplant, her heart had always seemed strong. How quickly we went from feeling that things were reasonably under control to realizing that things were totally out of control, at least totally out of our control.

The medical staff stabilized her and transferred her up to the Intensive Care Unit. I can't tell you how many times I had been in that ICU visiting family members from the church I pastored. But this was different. I wasn't visiting. This was my daughter. I was the one needing to be visited. My family was the one needing pastoral care.

After spending most of the afternoon in ICU, Kara seemed to be stable and her vital signs seemed strong; so I stepped out of her room for a few minutes while my wife stayed with her. While I was in one of the side rooms, a Code Blue alert sounded throughout the ICU. I knew it was for Kara. I went back into the ICU, and there were doctors and nurses surrounding Kara's bed. She had gone into cardiac arrest and the medical staff was doing everything they could to bring her back. However, as hard as they tried, on Monday evening, September 13, 2004, Kara Dawn Erickson's life on this earth came to an end much too soon, and she entered into the presence of her Lord and Savior Jesus Christ.

In the hours leading up to Kara's death and the days and weeks and months that followed, our family was cared for, loved and ministered to in ways that are hard to express in words. Throughout our journey with Kara, God surrounded us with a network of family and friends who helped us, supported us, prayed for us, encouraged us and did whatever they could to show the love of God in our times of need. Even to this day, we still get sympathy cards from people who remember Kara's life and the day of her homegoing.

As my wife and I stood next to Kara's lifeless body lying on the hospital bed, we prayed that God would use her death for His honor and glory. As hard as it was, we trusted God's sovereignty in life, and we wanted to trust His sovereignty in death. We had seen Him use Kara's struggles in life for His glory, now we wanted to see

Him use her death as well.

It wouldn't take long for God to answer our prayers. At Kara's funeral five days later, two of her closest friends would come to faith in Jesus Christ. Kara's boyfriend/soon to be fiancé, demonstrated an amazing spiritual maturity at her funeral that would set the stage for a life of devotion to Christ in spite of this huge loss. Our loss also would enable us to minister to others who would lose a child.

In the years that followed Kara's death, we have often been asked, "How did you handle it?" "Did you get angry with God?" Our response has always been, "As hard as it was to lose our daughter, we trusted in God, believing that He knew more about the whys than we would ever know or understand." God blessed us to be Kara's parents and to care for her for almost 26 years. After that, He took over and she is now fully healed. We have a sovereign God in whom we can trust no matter what. In the words of Job as he answered the Lord in his time of grief, "I know that you can do all things, and that no purpose of yours can be thwarted" (Job 42:2).

Shortly after Job's tragic losses, he cried out, ""Naked I came from my mother's womb, and naked shall I return. The Lord gave, and the Lord has taken away; blessed be the name of the Lord." (Job 1:21). The Lord gave us Kara on October 17, 1978 and the Lord took her home to heaven on September 13, 2004. Blessed be the name of the Lord.

A Psalm for Reflection

Psalm 30

I will exalt you, LORD, for you rescued me.
You refused to let my enemies triumph over me.
O LORD my God, I cried to you for help,
and you restored my health.
You brought me up from the grave, O LORD.
You kept me from falling into the pit of death.
Sing to the LORD, all you godly ones!
Praise his holy name.
For his anger lasts only a moment,
but his favor lasts a lifetime!
Weeping may last through the night,
but joy comes with the morning.
When I was prosperous, I said,
"Nothing can stop me now!"
Your favor, O LORD, made me secure as a mountain.
Then you turned away from me, and I was shattered.
I cried out to you, O LORD.
I begged the LORD for mercy, saying,
"What will you gain if I die,
if I sink into the grave?
Can my dust praise you?
Can it tell of your faithfulness?
Hear me, LORD, and have mercy on me.
Help me, O LORD."

*You have turned my mourning into joyful dancing.
You have taken away my clothes of mourning
and clothed me with joy,
that I might sing praises to you and not be silent.
O LORD my God, I will give you thanks forever! (NLT).*

CHAPTER EIGHT

Wash Your Face

> "Occasionally, weep deeply over the life you hoped would be. Grieve the losses. Feel the pain. Then wash your face. Trust God. And embrace the life you have."
>
> —John Piper

There was a hush. A hush so loud that everyone heard it. The baby had not made it through the night. No one dared tell the father. For the last week he refused persistent requests to, "Just eat something." He would not even wash, instead he lay on the ground weeping refusing to even change his clothes pleading with God over and over to spare his child's life. Now his son was dead. No one could bring themselves to break the news—afraid for the father's mental state fearing he would do something desperate. But, he already knew. He heard the whispers. "Is the child dead?" He asked.

"He is dead," they replied

"Then David got up from the ground. After he had washed, put on lotions and changed his clothes, he went into the house of the

Lord and worshiped," (2 Samuel 12:19-20 NIV). Why? His attendants asked him.

"Why are you acting this way?""While the child was alive, you fasted and wept, but now that the child is dead, you get up and eat?" (2 Samuel 12:21 NIV).

"Can I bring him back again?" David responds. "I will go to him, but he will not return to me. Then David comforted his wife Bathsheba, and he went to her and made love to her. She gave birth to a son, and they named him Solomon. The LORD loved him; and because the LORD loved him, he sent word through Nathan the prophet to name him Jedidiah (which means loved by the Lord or friend of God)" (2 Samuel 12:23-24 NIV parenthesis added)

I love the meaning behind a name. The name Solomon means peace. It is derived from the word Shalom.[22] What a lovely name for someone born after tragedy and loss. This story of loss includes a glimpse of comfort. It is a wonderful picture of moving forward in loss, even loss that came about due to sin. Can we bring our loved one back? No, can we go to them some day? David found hope in the knowledge that, yes, he would see his infant son again one day. Does life continue? Yes, and it should. You will need to get up again like David did. He rose from his grief and after washing went straight to the source of all comfort—worshiping in the house of God. Then he comforted his wife. Eventually they had another child and just like Eve found comfort in Seth's birth after Abel was killed, Bathsheba was also comforted by the birth of an additional child.

Comfort, it can be a choice. Do you choose to get up, wash your face, worship, comfort others and allow others to comfort you? The comfort is there, but it is partly our responsibility to choose to *accept* comfort when it is offered, something that this current culture is not always ready to do. We often like to wallow in our pain picking at our wounds instead of allowing them to heal.

I cannot forget the day a lady called to cancel her newspaper subscription, understandably because she did not know anyone in the tiny town where I had reopened a small, local paper. Our conversation quickly turned to more than a simple cancellation. Her husband had generously purchased a subscription purely out of support for me, a young woman business owner and friend. I had known her husband for several years as we volunteered together in a weekly ministry. I had never met his wife. She was known as someone who preferred to stay home, so when she called to cancel the subscription after her husband's death it was the first time I had ever spoken with her.

My heart broke for her. I have never lost a spouse, so I have no idea what that is like; but I have experienced grief and know that it can hurt so deeply. During our short conversation I shared my sympathies with her, as her husband was someone I really admired. "I have also experienced grief in my life," I said towards the end of our conversation hoping that might be a bridge of comfort for her. So many times I have found comfort from people who have gone through grief and opened up to share their stories with me, so my intent with the comment was purely one of solidarity. But, I quickly found out that my words were not taken as I had hoped.

I was told in no uncertain terms that the pain of losing a

husband was much worse than any other type of grief. My friend's wife told me that she had lost her mother and this recent loss was so much worse. I quietly gave my condolences again, and as I hung up the phone a wave of sadness filled me. "How do we comfort each other?" I thought. Sometimes trying just seems to make it worse. It was not my intention to compare pains, just sympathize and relate. But the conversation was a reminder that not everyone is at a place of being able to accept comfort.

It is so easy for pain to be seen as something that must be measured and if one person's pain is considered less painful or different then someone else's experience it is disregarded instead of being seen as a parallel road coming alongside in one's journey for healing. Attempting to offer comfort is difficult. It is easy to feel afraid to say anything because oftentimes we do say the wrong thing and then where does that leave you? Broken—we are all broken. It can be easy when someone offers a soft shoulder or an understanding ear to take it the wrong way. Of course, everyone's pain is unique. No one can understand exactly what someone else is going through, but does that mean we should never allow others to offer the comfort of sharing their journeys of grief with us? Sharing a journey of grief

> *It is so easy for pain to be seen as something that must be measured and if one person's pain is considered less painful or different then someone else's experience it is disregarded instead of being seen as a parallel road coming alongside in one's journey for healing.*

is not saying, "I have all the answers, or I know exactly what you are feeling or going through," it is just saying, "I have also faced the emotion stab of loss; not that the wound was bigger or smaller than yours—but my life has also been touched by death's sting. Let us walk this road together"

It is time to stop comparing pain, especially the pain of grief. When it comes to the lack of usefulness of comparing pain, Author Maggie Combs points out on an episode of The Podcast Worthy, "When my kid falls down on his bike, I don't come up to my son and say, 'you think this is pain, I gave birth to you and you were ten pounds.' We say, 'I know what pain feels like. I know what suffering is, so I just want to come alongside you and weep with you and be sad together. And then find the goodness of the gospel in our pain.'"[23]

Comparison of pains and pushing away comfort can be seen when people start to rate loss. It is seen in unhelpful ideas (sometimes expressed in words, sometimes in thoughts) ideas like a miscarriage should hurt less then a stillbirth. Why compare? Pain is pain. A life was lost.. We do not need to convince the world that we are hurting more than anyone else is. We do not need to think that we are not in a position to be able to offer comfort because the pain we have faced is less than the pain someone else is facing. Times of grief should not be a time for comparison. Times of grief are also not a time to push away comfort even when that comfort is awkwardly given. Let us give each other grace, and choose to look for and appreciate the comforting moments and comforting arms that God sends.

God sent a special comfort to Isaac after he lost his mother,

Sarah. I love the verse in Genesis 24:67 that beautifully describes the intimate moment that Isaac took Rebekah, as his wife, "Isaac brought her into the tent of his mother Sarah, and he married Rebekah. So she became his wife, and he loved her; and Isaac was comforted after his mother's death (NIV). Comforted—a new love coming at a time of loss. What a beautiful picture of how God so often brings unique comforts even in times of loss. What if Isaac had said, "No, my mother just died. I'm not opening up my heart again. More pain might come." He would have been missing out on the special comfort that God had prepared for him coming at just the time when he needed it.

I have often seen this idea of pain and joy coming at the same time in the lives of those going through loss—the loss of a family member followed by an engagement or the birth of a child coming soon after the death of a loved one. Happy moments in the midst of trial coming almost hand in hand. Tears mixed with joy. The comfort is often there; it is just up to the individual whether they wish to embrace it or turn away.

Pushing away comfort can come in many forms like refusing to celebrate someone else's happiness because your pain feels too great. It can be avoiding a baby shower because your own arms are empty. I do not say this lightly. Acknowledge your grief. Say, yes this is hard. Do not force yourself to go if you are not yet in a place where you feel you are ready to do so. But, also do not stay away forever from events that remind you of your own loss. Sometimes the very things that you fear will bring the most pain can actually end up being a source of comfort.

My son was born after a very long labor. My mom, who used

to work as an OB nurse, told me his color did not look good. Since my husband is from Papua New Guinea, and I very much take after my mom's Dutch roots, I did not know what color to expect our son's skin to be. I told my mom not to worry. But, I was wrong. Grey is never a good color in a newborn. He had inhaled meconium into his lungs during the long labor, and his tiny lungs were not responding well. My little guy was put on oxygen and an IV was started before I even had the chance to try and nurse him. The hospital where I gave birth did not have a nursery so my not even one-day-old baby was transferred by ambulance across the road to the general hospital, and things did not look good. I was allowed to see him settled into the nursery but then told that I needed to return to the hospital where I had just given birth in order to be discharged.

One of the widows we work with stopped by the hospital with her young granddaughter and a freshly cooked dinner. I held on to her granddaughter so tightly, wishing of course that I could be holding my little boy. My sweet baby did recover and after five days that felt like five weeks, we were able to bring sweet Trevor home.[24] A baby brought me comfort in a moment when I did not know if I would ever be able to hold my baby again. It was a gift from God in the moment that I needed it, and I am so glad that I embraced that comforting gift of holding someone else's baby in that hard moment.

One of the other ladies who married into my husband's tribe also had a baby boy around the same time I did. I remember the day my son got his two-month shots. We were at a gathering of the tribe, and everyone wanted to see Trevor or hold him especially, since his mixed race status makes him somewhat of a novelty. I remember wishing I could just hide away with the other new mom and let my little guy get an undisturbed nap like her son was.

Tragically, her baby passed away a few months later. I sat on the grass in the village watching as his tiny coffin was decorated with freshly picked flowers thinking just how sad it all was. I wished that life was not so painful. I wished I could fix it or make it better, and yet I was so powerless to do anything but sit there on the grass with the rest of the family. I did not see the little boy's mom again for several months. The next time I saw her the first thing she did was grab Trevor and give him a huge hug. She kept doing that every time I would see her. I was a bit surprised as I am sure she was thinking of her own sweet boy who would have been around Trevor's age. I was impressed with her ability to embrace comfort by holding someone else's baby instead of avoiding what could have been a painful reminder.

I saw this mom again earlier in the year at another tribal gathering. My heart was happy to see her now holding a baby girl around the same age as my daughter. What a sweet comfort. I hope our girls will become friends as their lives occasionally cross, and I'll never forget the little boy, her second born son, who we all wish could have stayed with us longer on this earth. Like David, I am sure she looks forward to the day that she will be united once again with her precious child

"He was despised and rejected by men, a Man of sorrows and acquainted with grief." —Isaiah 53:3

She Took Her First Breath in Heaven

By Tara Amis

EXCITEDLY, WE WAITED for the doctor to find our 16-week-old baby's heartbeat. No luck.

"That's ok," he said as he pulled out a portable ultrasound. We saw a sweet head, but still no heartbeat.

"Oh I'm worrying you! I'm sorry, don't worry. We will just set up a full ultrasound and see what's going on," the doctor assured us. I sent a friend a quick text, "I'm in the waiting room waiting for an ultrasound, couldn't find the heartbeat. I'm sure everything is fine; but please pray just in case." I truly believed nothing was wrong.

I wasn't worried; I wasn't one of those women who had miscarriages. I couldn't wait to see my baby. Maybe we could find out the gender early! As we were called back the ultrasound tech got everything set up. We looked at the monitor and saw a head, beautiful body, arms and legs. Everything looked perfect. The doctor stepped in and they quickly turned the machine off. He looked me in the eyes, with the most compassionate, pained expression and said, "I'm sorry. There is no heartbeat. Your baby is dead. It looks like the baby stopped growing about a week ago."

I didn't understand. I couldn't comprehend. I had two beautiful boys. At the time, my oldest was four and my middle son was two.

While waiting for the surgery, my sister came and got our two-year-old while my parents and pastors stayed with us. I went into the surgical suite crying, "I don't want this. I want my baby!" I needed everyone to know that this was a nightmare. When I woke up I was crying again, however, I had a song in my head. "Tis Jesus the first and the last. Whose spirit shall guide us safe home. I will praise Him for all that has passed and trust Him for all that is to come."[25] We had taught the children this song at our Bible Study Fellowship group that year and God put it in my head as the first comfort. I was able to stop crying. It was like a hug for my soul— *my first gift.*

The next day was my sister's birthday. I struggled to be a positive person, but I tried! Two weeks later it was my birthday. I had no desire to celebrate. My husband took me to Hot Springs, Arkansas to try to help bring healing. It was good. We talked and read through Job. We read several Psalms. During and after our trip we had many conversations about salvation, life, death, about healing, about God's plans and about sin. During our trip we were intimate for the first time since our loss. I share this because I didn't know how hard that would be. My husband and I had never struggled in this area. We love each other very deeply, but I felt like I had let him down.

We didn't know why this had happened; yet I blamed myself even though you have to tell everyone that you don't. It's pretty impossible not to. Your head may know this as truth but your heart struggles. Over the next few weeks, I struggled to keep the house clean, kids taken care of and all my responsibilities managed. Sometimes I felt like my heart weighed 50 pounds, other times I felt like it was exploding. There were times I was crying so hard I thought I would cry my insides out. We had an area in our bedroom that was kind of random—not a closet (too big) and no door. The only way to get to it was through our room. We decided it would be the perfect space for a nursery. I remember sitting against that empty wall crying, sobbing and sometimes just sitting.

We held a memorial service where we sang worship songs and read scripture. My dad spoke about loss, and we mourned with our friends and family. We found comfort in a song called "Zion" by Kings Kaleidoscope and had it played during the memorial. The memorial was beautiful—I had pictures, candles and things to hold. It seems so trivial but being able to have something from our daughter's pregnancy meant everything. The doctor was able to give us a plaque with her footprints, and I had two pictures of me while pregnant and one set of ultrasound pictures. We named her Isabella which means consecrated to God. I thought of Hannah giving up Samuel and knew that just like God had a plan for Samuel, He had a plan for Isabella. Psalm 139:16 says "Your eyes saw my unformed substance; in your book were written, every one of them, the days that were formed for me, when as yet there was none of them." This was the verse we gave to her. It soothed my heart—*my second gift*.

We decided to try getting pregnant again and planned and paid for a trip to Florida. Then my husband lost his job. He decided being a nurse wasn't for him and wanted to do something else. We stopped trying to get pregnant but decided we should keep our travel plans since we had already paid for everything. Zack found an opportunity to take a night class to learn computer coding. The class started the day after we planned to come back from our trip. The last day to sign up was the day we found out about the class. It felt like it was God's timing. Zack successfully changed careers and now works full time doing programming and teaches the class he once took.

We left for Florida and really felt healing. Our boys were so excited to see the beach. We were there for a week, but I knew something was different the first day of the trip. I was pregnant again. I thought I would be happy. When we were trying before my husband lost his job, I wanted to be pregnant, but now I was not excited. I wanted to be, but I just wasn't. We went through the motions. A friend of mine took beautiful pictures of our family on the beach announcing our pregnancy.

I had started learning how to embroider on that trip, so I picked up a few onesies, more thread and went to town creating rainbow baby designs. It was soothing. I could focus on making something beautiful when all I could think about was "How are we going to afford this baby? How will we buy food? How will we get through this time?" God provided. Zack worked three jobs while taking the programming class. Our church helped us financially when needed. My parents owned the house we were living in and graciously let us pay rent when we were able too. We had food stamps and Medicaid. My mom would come help with the boys, and I would go to my parent's house when Zack was in class so that I wasn't alone.

I was incredibly sick during my pregnancy. We were told two eggs had been fertilized. One was much smaller than the other and was eventually reabsorbed. Hearing this I felt like I had miscarried all over again. The doctor tried to tell me that I shouldn't feel that way, but I can't believe that. I believe we will meet that baby in heaven too.

I started going to counseling after my sister got into a terrible car accident. I remember her saying, "I was so worried I was going to die."

I thought, "I wouldn't be worried. Dying wouldn't be the end of the world." I would see my baby. I didn't want to die, but I felt like it would be ok if I did. My husband was unable to help. He didn't know what to say and didn't feel the pain the same way I did. I needed someone I could talk to who wouldn't judge or be emotional. This isn't to say people didn't want to help me. I had so many people who wanted to lift me up which was wonderful, however counseling felt safe. With counseling, I didn't have to worry about hurting my counselor's feelings. I could just talk. God blessed me with a Godly woman whose husband was a pastor. She knew I trusted God and that I knew He had a plan. I knew so much in my head, but my emotions were going crazy.

I struggled with flashbacks. She taught me about grounding techniques. With these techniques I was then able to remember the events without being stuck in them. My counselor also helped me become excited about my pregnancy. She helped me work through all my thoughts. The biggest was, "How do I love this new person while still wishing I had Isabella?" I felt if I was excited about my new little one, then I wasn't honoring Isabella; and if I was mourning Isabella, I wasn't glad about my new pregnancy. These emotions, I learned, were not mutually exclusive! I could grieve Isabella and wish she was with us and still be so blessed by my youngest. During this time, I read Jeremiah 1:5 "Before I formed you in the womb I knew you, and before you were born I consecrated you; I appointed you a prophet to the nations." We named our third son Jeremiah because God knew he needed to be born and had such plans that we had to go through our grief with Isabella.

We learned I have an autoimmune disorder called Antiphospholipid Syndrome which is what caused the miscarriage. My body makes small blood clots that don't hurt me, but they were enough to cause our sweet Isabella to lose her blood supply and pass away. There was nothing I could have done, and our first two boys were truly a miracle since I've always had this we just didn't know it. During Jeremiah's pregnancy I had to take daily injections of a blood thinner. By the 34th week of my pregnancy I had gestational diabetes, pubic symphysis and never-ending morning sickness. Jeremiah always measured huge, and I had a lot of extra fluid which didn't help with my comfort.

Then I got a kidney stone. Of course being 34 weeks pregnant they couldn't do an x-ray so there was no way to confirm and no pain medicine was possible. After I passed the stone in the hospital they told me I would feel much better. I didn't. Zack and I both were diagnosed with the flu. I had a doctor come and talked about delivering early if we had to. He said I most likely had preeclampsia again, and if I couldn't get my blood pressure down (which was sky high since I just passed a kidney stone) we would have to deliver early. But, we wanted Jeremiah to stay in for as long as possible. A few days later I was 35.3 weeks, and my blood pressure never went down. On February 12, 2019 I had our rainbow baby. He spent 3.5

weeks in the NICU which was its own complicated story. I've used this term "rainbow baby" but never explained it. A rainbow baby refers to a baby born after a miscarriage. The expression comes from the phrase "A rainbow at the end of the storm." After all that pain, I was finally able to hold my new miracle. My joy. My rainbow at the end of my storm—*our 3rd gift, Jeremiah.*

I'm not healed. I don't think I will ever be completely healed. Writing these words has been through many tears. But one day I will hold my sweet baby. I will see her face and hold her hand. I will find out the color of her hair and eyes. I have red hair, so I imagine she does too. This is part of living in a sinful world. This pain of death is not because of anything specific we have done wrong, but sin is separation from God and death is a part of that. Isabella is not separated from God. She took her first breath in heaven. She learned to walk at the feet of God. She never felt pain or fear. She is not sad. She never had a cold. She will never feel these things. What a blessing! We are blessed to have had her for 16 weeks and to have the joy of knowing that, one day, we will see her. God is not done giving us gifts. I was given the gift of Isabella. I held her in my womb. I will forever hold her in my heart. I will hold my forever little one in my arms one day, and until then I have my three sweet boys and look forward to one day adopting a little girl. I am unable to safely have more children, so we plan to walk the road of adoption. This will come with its own losses. My sweet future daughter will have to face the loss of her birth parents. For whatever reason, she will be separated; but now I know loss too. I understand pain, and I will be better able to walk that road with her—*my 4th gift.*

A Psalm for Reflection

Psalm 31

In you, Lord, I have taken refuge;
let me never be put to shame;
in your righteousness deliver me!.
incline your ear to me;
rescue me speedily!
Be a rock of refuge for me,
a strong fortress to save me!

For you are my rock and my fortress;
and for your name's sake you lead and guide me;
you take me out of the net they had hidden for me,
for you are my refuge.
Into your hands I commit my spirit;
you have redeemed me, O LORD, faithful God.

I hate those who pay regard to worthless idols,
but I trust in the LORD.
I will rejoice and be glad in your steadfast love,
because you have seen my affliction;
you have known the distress of my soul,
and you have not delivered me into the hands of the enemy;
you have set my feet in a broad place.

Be gracious to me, O LORD, for I am in distress;
my eye is wasted from grief;
my soul and my body also.
For my life is spent with sorrow,

and my years with sighing;
my strength fails because of my iniquity,
and my bones waste away.

Because of all my adversaries
I have become a reproach,
especially to my neighbors,
and an object of dread to my acquaintances;
those who see me in the street flee from me.
I have been forgotten like one who is dead;
I have become like a broken vessel.
For I hear many whispering of many—
Terror on every side!—
as they scheme together against me
as they plot to take my life.

But I trust in you, O LORD;
I say, "You are my God."
My times are in your hand;
rescue me from the hands of
my enemies and from my persecutors!
Make your face shine on your servant;
save me in your steadfast love!
O LORD, let me not be put to shame,
for I call upon you;
let the wicked be put to shame
let them go silently to Sheol.
Let the lying lips be mute,
which peak insolently
against the righteous in pride and contempt.

Oh, how abundant is your goodness,

*which you have stored up for those who fear you
and worked for those who take refuge in you,
in the sight of the children of mankind!
In the cover of your presence you hide them
from the plots of men;
you store them in your shelter
from the strife of tongues.*

*Blessed be the LORD,
for he has wondrously shown his steadfast love to me
when I was in a besieged city.
I had said in my alarm,
"I am cut off from your sight."
But you heard the voice of my pleas for mercy
when I cried to you for help.*

*Love the LORD, all you his saints!
The LORD preserves the faithful
but abundantly repays the one who acts in pride.
Be strong, and let your heart take courage,
all you who wait for the LORD!*

CHAPTER NINE

The Ministry of Pain

> "One of the hardest things to do when you are hurting is to think about someone else. But one of the best things to do when you are hurting is to think about somebody else."
>
> –Dr. Tony Evans

I had no idea when I signed up to run my first 5K that the race I chose was billed as Missouri's toughest 5K. Oops, maybe not the smartest choice for a runner whose last track event was in first grade. At the encouragement of a friend, I mailed in my registration fee, downloaded the Couch to 5K app and showed up with hundreds of other runners all dressed in our bright orange shirts. We pinned on our crisp black and white bib numbers and ran/walked 3.1 miles of Missouri's hilly terrain. Hoops for Life- a tough race for a tough cause, was organized by the parents of Sahara Aldridge, a basketball-loving girl who passed away from brain cancer in 2007. This event has since raised thousands of dollars for Lucile Packard Children's Hospital at Stanford University, a place that helped Sahara during her own fight against cancer.[26] I was touched by Sahara's parents' strength and how they honored their precious daughter in such a special way by working to raise money to help others fighting a disease that continues to devastate so many lives.

Pain. We can never stop it. Living in a broken, sin-filled world which is sadly rife with disease, trauma and death—pain is inevitable. It is a curse originating in the fall that will not be lifted until all things are once again made new. So the question is, where will the inevitable pain that you experience in life take you? Are there any ways that the pain you have experienced can help you lift up others who are experiencing a similar sorrow? In *The Magnet*, by Mary McDonald, Mary's therapist tells her, "We can be broken like glass and cut others with the shards from our trauma, or we can be broken like bread and nourish others like Jesus' broken body…The Bread of Heaven."[27] How profound—such a beautiful picture of the ministry of pain. God uses our broken hearts and broken stories, stories full of emotional scars. We can be cracked vessels willing to continue pouring out and administer healing just as Jesus did ministering to others even up to His last breath.

How will you choose to use your pain? My friend Amanda, who shared her story after chapter one, collected magazines and books for the families in the waiting rooms of cancer hospitals. What a practical idea. I never would have even thought to do something like that because I have never been in a waiting room while a family member faced cancer treatments. She saw a unique way to bring comfort and also honor the memory of her mom and all that she went through because she, herself, had spent hours in waiting rooms.

When you lose someone, you will often find that you have been given a new ministry—the ministry of ministering to others in their pain. It is a ministry that few would actually choose, even though it is one of the most powerful ministries there is. It is often the case that as you help others through their grief, or look for ways to bring something positive out of a very negative situation, this can be a way for your own soul to begin healing.

My mom helps lead GriefShare groups. She also makes an effort to go to funerals, even of people she might not know very well. It may not be easy to be near so much pain, but her presence is often a comfort. Several years ago she went to a funeral of one of her students who was killed when hit by a train. Even though she had never met her student's mother before, in the receiving line she briefly explained that she had also lost a daughter. The girl's mom thanked her for coming, saying that knowing this, and just seeing my mom standing in front of her, gave her hope that she too would one day get through this difficult period.

With the ministry of pain, the object should not necessarily be to "fix" a person or a situation, but more to just be with those needing comfort, and to "weep with those who weep" Romans 12:15.[28] We should seek to minister in a way that reflects love and patience and points people to the One who gives true peace. It is important to realize that this is an arena of ministry where you will likely see people in their most vulnerable states mentally, emotionally, spiritually and sometimes even physically.

As hard as it is to walk through pain, it does allow for ministering in a way that those who have not personally done so cannot do as well. A personal experience with pain often allows one to reach deeper places and break down carefully built facades because you become one who knows. The naivety and bliss of the ignorant has shattered making way for new levels of growth and understanding.

Getting to that place—that place of effectiveness, that place of ministry, that place of being stretched to a point of new growth is often painful; so in our selfish flesh we do not want it. "We all want a testimony," Joanna Weaver writes, "But we would rather skip the test that gives us one."[29] Just think of your favorite book or movie. A good story has conflict, trials, pain and growth. If I pick up a book and it is all sunshine and roses, I'll be honest, I do not waste my time with it for two reasons. First, it does not feel authentic to me as I do not see perfect lives in real life and if a book does not reflect real life (and real life this side of heaven involves pain) why read it? Secondly, I want to see growth and change in a character if I'm going to invest time into reading a story; and growth and change rarely happen without struggle. There is this odd dynamic in modern society of wanting the white picket fence dream—a good marriage, the exact number of children (of course only in the genders that you prefer), no health challenges, no

> A personal experience with pain often allows one to reach deeper places and break down carefully built facades because you become one who knows. The naivety and bliss of the ignorant has shattered making way for new levels of growth and understanding.

financial struggles, just a good, happy life well documented with carefully filtered Instagram posts.

But, does this lead to a more holy life? Is this what God has in mind? Are we willing to let go and let the child born with a disability, learning challenge or challenging personality grow us as a family or a community? Are we able to see the good and the opportunity for ministry that happens beyond our carefully planned out dreams and goals? Will the death of a loved one break us to the point where we pull completely into ourselves, withdrawing and losing trust in the One who is fully good because life is no longer going how we planned it? Many times God's ways are *not* our ways. His plans are *not* our plans—and that, my friend, is actually a good thing.

My husband is the fifth boy in his family and by that point his parents really wanted a girl. But, I'm sure glad that he was born a boy. God had great plans for his life that maybe did not line up with his parents' wishes at the time (they did have a girl after him) but fit with God's bigger and better plans. Sometimes we will be called in life to mourn a dream or a desire that does not make sense at the time. Why won't God just give me the spouse I so desperately desire, the daughter I have always longed for, the job that would make life so much easier? All good things but trust—trust that there is a reason, a bigger picture. Mourn the loss but then ask how can the lessons that God is teaching me be used to minister to others? What you go through, especially the hard things, will open doors for ministry if you allow it to. Suffering is one of the most powerful tools of reaching out that there is as messy and painful as it can be.

Permission to Mourn

In one of my all-time favorite fiction series, the ever deeply-feeling Anne Shirley is newly married and living with her country doctor husband on a rural Canadian island. She is drawn to a kindred spirit, she feels, a young lady named Leslie whose life is marked by tragedy. Leslie was pressured into marrying a spiteful man who was later injured to the point of being mentally affected. Anne watches as her new friend cares for her now child-like husband, living in near poverty and not able to enjoy many of the joys that a woman full of youth, beauty and ambition should be enjoying. But, as much as Anne tries to connect with her neighbor, Anne feels that there is an unspoken wall. Anne's motives for friendship are pure, but she constantly feels held at arm's length as she attempts to get close to Leslie. It is not until Anne loses a baby shortly after birth that this wall crumbles. "I hope you won't misunderstand me if I say something" Leslie finally confides in Anne. "I was grieved to the core of my heart when you lost your baby; and if I could have saved her for you by cutting off one of my hands I would have done it. But your sorrow has brought us closer together. Your perfect happiness isn't a barrier any longer. Oh, don't misunderstand, dearest—I'm NOT glad that your happiness isn't perfect any longer—I can say that sincerely; but since it isn't, there isn't such a gulf between us."[30] Sorrow and loss broke through and the two, through pain, were able to fully share their lives together and bring comfort to each other.

Painful experiences come with the questions—how can I begin to heal? How can I use what I have been through to help others heal? These two questions can often go hand in hand as walking with others through their pain often helps heal one's own pain.

I first attended the training for leading the healing from trauma workshops that we have used with the widows we work with because a mentor of mine here in PNG had recently lost her daughter. In the midst of the pain she was processing, she organized a training in the city where we lived. Her pain was great, but she has used it as a catalyst, in many ways, from organizing healing from trauma workshops to starting a library in honor of her daughter in their village. Many people have now been blessed through these ministries, offerings flowing from much pain.

Some resent the growth that suffering can bring. "I am a more sensitive person, a more effective pastor, a more sympathetic counselor because of Arron's life and death then I would ever have been without it," Rabbi Kusner writes in regard to his son's death. "And I would give up all those gains in a second if I could have my son back."[31] This is an understandable sentiment. I think we all feel this about the pain we walk through if we are honest with ourselves. It is not easy to look past the hurt to see the good. Of course, we would have rather avoided that intense loss completely even though deep down we can see how it grows us.

Think of your favorite hymn. You will discover that most were birthed from places of pain when reading the back-story of what led someone to write. If Fanny Crosby had not been born blind would she have written an estimated 8,000 hymns and memorized large portions of scripture? Doubtfully, and yet her words, often written from a place of great suffering, continue to minister to so many. Her hymn "Safe in the Arms of Jesus" was sung at my sister's funeral, as I am sure it has been sung at many others bringing comfort to those facing fresh wounds of grief.

Permission to Mourn

Avoid it or embrace it, when walking down roads of suffering new doors of ministry will open. The choice is yours how to move forward. As discussed in the previous chapter, choosing comfort is a choice. There is a strange idea that seems to pop up in modern cultures that says, "no one else can understand my pain, so don't even try to comfort me." What a sad, lonely perspective. While I understand that each person grieves differently and yes, you don't know exactly what someone else is feeling as they process through pain, comforting each other and having someone say, "Yes, I'm walking a similar road," can be medicine for a lonely soul steeped in grief.

Like the negative example of Job's "friends" we need to be careful with what we say and maybe err on the side of saying less, but we are commanded to mourn and rejoice together. Note this verse does not say fix, lecture, blame or debate with those who are mourning, it says mourn and weep in community. Do not avoid. Do not feel that you need to have some kind of magic wisdom or feel better pill. Just weep over loss; a ministry that becomes easier and easier the more loss you face and empathy levels grow.

When I was pregnant with my daughter, Allyson, it was in the middle of Port Moresby's hottest months. I felt like I was constantly dripping in sweat and battling heat rashes that would just not go away. A friend of mine, who was also pregnant at the time, came over and I remember commiserating with her about the heat and the aches and pains of the third trimester. When I would say things to my husband like, "this baby's head feels like it is permanently stuck under my rib." I felt like I was complaining, but when my friend and I were talking, she totally understood because we were in the same situation. Nothing felt like a complaint, just a lot of "me too!" moments and, "I totally feel what you are saying." It was so comforting to have someone who got it because even though our experiences were not identical we were both in a similar situation, which made empathy easy.

A similar thing can happen when grieving together. Yes, individual experiences will differ, but there is comfort in knowing that other people have been there. Other people have felt what it is like to feel the vulnerability that comes with loss. Other people know what it is like to be laughing about a memory one minute and then sobbing the next. Other people have experienced the grief that comes with sorting through belongings and deciding what to keep and what to donate or sell. Other people know what it is like to have to call and cancel a favorite magazine or write out details to be put in a newspaper obituary. There is comfort in knowing that you are not the first person who has had to walk this journey. Reach out and grab some empathetic hands. Find a shoulder and some comforting arms to hold you when there are no words, but also be open to being a hand to hold for someone else. Together is often how one finds the strength to move forward.

> "Blessed be the God and Father of our Lord Jesus Christ, the Father of mercies and God of all comfort, who comforts us in all our afflictions, so that we will be able to comfort those who are in any affliction, with the comfort with which we ourselves are comforted by God."
> —2 Corinthians 1:3-4

I Know that Ache

By Barb Lamb

IN JUNE OF 1989, I first met my husband, Carter. There were dates and many long walks accompanied by long talks of life, our families, our interests and faith in God. He was dealing with the end of a five-year marriage, moving back to Illinois from Michigan and looking for somebody to date. The old saying, "You have to kiss a lot of toads before you meet the handsome prince," pretty much summed up my dating life prior to meeting Carter. Quickly, we both decided that we were perfect for each other.

In January of '90, he wasn't feeling well, so I encouraged him to go see a doctor for a check-up. Since we weren't living together at that point in time, I had no idea how many trips to the bathroom he made; otherwise, I probably would have guessed he was developing diabetes. By changing his diet and using insulin, we knew we could handle this health change together. Barely engaged, I attended a "diabetes class" with him at the local hospital, so we both would be informed about the illness.

On September 22, 1990, we were married, and survived the day without any hypoglycemic issues. Early married life included working together on home projects, traveling and eventually starting a family. Since I was already in my early thirties, "the biological clock" was ticking. Our daughter, Elise, was born in

October of 1992 and our son, AJ, was born in May of 1996. Life was pretty wonderful due to both of us having jobs and traveling with the kids, along with involvement in our local church.

In early 2000, Carter began complaining of hearing and vision issues. The vision issue was corrected easily, but he saw a variety of specialists to solve the mystery of what was going on with the hearing in his one ear. An ENT suggested a brain scan to check for possible tiny, benign tumors on his ear canal to see if this was the issue. The good news was, no benign tumors; the bad news was, they did find plaques, or lesions, on the brain. Sadly, Carter was officially diagnosed with multiple sclerosis.

Avonex was his first MS medication, which he handled well. Over time, he had more "flare ups" and his doctor switched him over to Copaxone. Carter and I agreed early on to still live our lives as "normally" as possible. We didn't want our kids to miss out on trying different sports and activities. However, Carter's MS eventually affected his mobility, and we transitioned from a cane, to a walker and to using a wheelchair over time. Chairlifts were installed in our two-story home, rather than moving into a ranch-style home. Remarkably, we just kept plugging along and trying to continue living as normal a life as possible.

Carter continued to work, and his employer actually had a small electric cart for him to use at work. Eventually, he started to have days that included either hypoglycemic episodes or just plain exhaustion from the MS. When keeping him safe at work was becoming difficult, his employer suggested he medically retire in 2009.

Again, we just kept plugging along, attending our children's events and taking short trips as best as we could. There were days that we learned that extreme heat and MS don't go together well. There were days we didn't monitor his blood sugar levels very well. Several men from church would come and check on him at lunchtime a few days a week, or they took Carter to his medical appointments for me. This allowed me to not miss work as often.

Spring of 2010, everything changed for our family. Carter went into the hospital with a urinary tract infection for a few days. The combination of his two illnesses along with heavy doses of antibiotics, left him pretty weak. Doctors suggested that he attend a rehabilitation facility to receive both physical and occupational therapy. Sadly, Carter missed AJ's Junior High graduation. This was the first big family event that he had to miss.

Thus began an ongoing cycle in our lives…no matter how hard we tried to keep Carter well fed, well hydrated and "moving," he would wind up with frequent urinary tract infections. We took him to the ER; he would then be admitted to the hospital for a few days. Sometimes, he was then sent to a rehab/nursing facility for PT and OT; other times he came home. Because he was so sedentary, he dealt with pressure sores on his bottom that eventually required special wound care procedures and surgeries. Eventually, he had a permanent catheter placed in his abdomen and dealt with kidney stones. Later, he exhibited seizures when an infection settled into his body. Carter had twenty-six hospital stays and nine rehab/nursing home stays in 5 ½ years.

Eventually, we had a hospital bed installed at home with a special air mattress to help with the pressure sores. Over time, I learned various "home health care nursing skills." There were home health care nurses, PTs, OTs and assigned caregivers here on a regular basis. Our dear friends from church, Gary and Sandy, voluntarily went out of their way to help us on a regular basis.

Once, in the early stages of all of these hospital visits, my son asked, "What is God trying to teach us through all of this, Mom?" I sighed and said, "Perseverance?" I now knew that I needed to rely not just on our wonderful friends from church that helped us, but on God and his Word.

The first Bible passage that I began reading daily was Isaiah 40:29-31:

He gives strength to the weary and increases the power of the weak. Even youths grow tired and weary, and young men stumble and fall; but those who hope in the Lord will renew their strength. They will soar on wings like eagles; they will run and not grow weary, they will walk and not be faint (NIV).

It gave me encouragement and strength to get through each day. I kept working throughout all of this. (We needed health insurance!) I eventually added to my daily list: Isaiah 41: 10, 13, Deuteronomy 31:8, 2 Corinthians 12:9-10 and of course, James 1:2-4. These were the "basics" for the start of my day, every day.

Carter went to the hospital on August 19, 2017, with not only another UTI and seizures, but also pneumonia as well. His oxygen levels weren't superb, but would show occasional improvement. He spent his 58th birthday in the hospital; and I made sure that Elise, AJ, his mom and sisters came to visit him…just in case he was not coming home with us. Remarkably, he improved enough to go to a nursing facility for a few days on Friday, September 15th. Elise and I went down to visit AJ, as it was his last "family weekend" at college that fall. When we returned Sunday evening, the care facility called to say they were transporting him back to the hospital. Something wasn't quite right. When I got to the hospital on Monday, his pneumonia had returned. The next day, after talking with both physicians who were working on him, it was confirmed that recurring pneumonia was probably "the beginning of the end" for Carter's time with us. I didn't cry at the hospital in front of the doctors and staff, but I sure did lose it that evening at home.

At the end of September, Carter returned home to his special hospital bed. He was put on hospice care. Knowing that another bout with pneumonia was not worth another trip to the hospital, I learned how to properly feed Carter via a feeding tube at home and take care of him as best I could. Our caregiver, Joe, was with him during the day and I kept working.

Carter stayed in hospice care at home until December 18th. On that morning, his hospice care nurse called me since he had been struggling when she saw him earlier that day. I left lesson plans at my school for the next few days and shared the news with my coworkers that I wouldn't be in for the rest of the week. When I got home and asked his nurse, "Are we looking at a day or two?" her reply was, "No honey, I think we're looking at hours."

Yikes! AJ was home because he had just finished finals week at college. Elise was still at school, so I called her. She arrived home ASAP. Our dear friend, Sandy, from church, came over for emotional support. I phoned his mom, sisters, a few other friends and our pastor from church. The "regular" hospice nurse reported to the "final hours" hospice nurse. Joe, his caregiver, said his goodbyes to Carter before he left for the day.

Reflecting back on the evening, Elise, AJ and I agree it was pretty surreal. Visits from one of his sisters, the pastors, church elders and also Gary. One of the pastors reminded us to order some dinner, so we ordered pizza. Elise, AJ and I each took some time alone with Carter at his bedside. Instead of MeTV (Carter's favorite cable channel), we put on a classic rock music channel that eerily played songs such as "Time for Me to Fly" or other songs by his favorite classic rock artists. Then the nurse informed us that it was almost his time…all three of us, and Sandy, stood arm in arm by his side and just cried and cried. It was 8:02 PM when Carter left his earthly home and went to his heavenly home.

The visitation and funeral were equally surreal. We felt extremely blessed and loved by so many that attended. All three of us shared a reading during the service. The worst part was following the casket outside and hearing the final slam of the hearse's rear door. The tears returned again. I cannot even recall which pallbearer's shoulder I buried my face into at that moment.

Elise, AJ and I continue to go out to dinner on Father's Day and Carter's birthday, choosing a favorite restaurant or a favorite meal of his. We order pizza for dinner on December 18th. Sharing laughs and stories and playing lots of classic rock music is how we honor Carter. I don't watch MeTV very often; it's too painful for me. I think of him multiple times a day, almost every day. I try to dwell on the good memories and realize he is in heaven and in no more pain—no more injections, no pills, no bedsores and no feeding tubes. I do miss him. Going through a Griefshare class and a Growth Group program have helped in many ways, but I still miss him. My heart is heavy every time a friend loses a loved one…I ache because I know what the ache is like. The ache never really leaves, it just changes over time, yet we will continue to persevere with our lives as best as we can.

A Psalm for Reflection

Psalm 86

Incline your ear, O LORD, and answer me,
for I am poor and needy.
Preserve my life, for I am godly;
save your servant, who trusts in you—you are my God.
Be gracious to me, O Lord,
for to you do I cry all the day.
Gladden the soul of your servant,
for to you, O Lord, do I lift up my soul.
For you, O Lord, are good and forgiving,
abounding in steadfast love to all who call upon you.
Give ear, O LORD, to my prayer
listen to my plea for grace.
In the day of my trouble I call upon you,
for you answer me.
There is none like you among the gods, O Lord,
nor are there any works like yours.
All the nations you have made shall come
and worship before you, O Lord,
and shall glorify your name.
For you are great and do wondrous things;
you alone are God.
Teach me your way, O LORD,
that I may walk in your truth;
unite my heart to fear your name.
I give thanks to you, O Lord my God, with my whole heart,
and I will glorify your name forever.
For great is your steadfast love toward me;

you have delivered my soul from the depths of Sheol.
O God, insolent men have risen up against me
a band of ruthless men seeks my life,
and they do not set you before them.
But you, O Lord, are a God merciful and gracious,
slow to anger and abounding in steadfast love and faithfulness.
Turn to me and be gracious to me
give your strength to your servant,
and save the son of your maidservant.
Show me a sign of your favor,
that those who hate me may see and be put to shame
because you, LORD, have helped me and comforted me.

CHAPTER TEN

Stop! Don't Say That

> "Believe it or not, one of the best things you can say is, 'I don't know what to say.' I know it sounds weak. But that's the beauty of it. It reflects humility. It communicates that you don't presume to have words that would make the loss okay. It esteems their loss as being too great to minimize by mere sentiment."
>
> —Nancy Guthrie (What Grieving People Wish You Knew)

One of my son's classmates died very suddenly last week due to an accident. He was just four years old. As we sat with his family the first two days after his passing I was once again overwhelmed with the reality that, especially in some situations, there are just no words to make it better. What do you say to the young mom holding her son's body sobbing for him to wake up? What do you say to a grandfather in the midst of such shock and disbelief struggling to accept the unthinkable? Even phrases like "I'm so sorry for your loss" can feel so inadequate. So we sat with the family. My husband helped them sort out logistics of needed paperwork from the hospital and transporting the body to the morgue. We sat, brought food for the family, drank coffee with them, listened when they felt like talking, shed tears together and allowed the little boy's auntie to just hold my son as she wept for the little boy she loved and already missed deeply. The second time we came to the haus krai, a group of the mom's coworkers also came with food and to just sit with the family. When we, and the coworkers, were getting ready to leave, the young boy's grandpa thanked us for coming and said (translated from Tok Pisin), "We find this a difficult reality to accept. Thank you for coming and sharing our sorrow with us." Sharing sorrow, his words touched me. Yes, there are no words that can reverse the pain, but we can be present as a community and help share the immensely overwhelming burden of sorrow.

It is likely that if you have lost someone close to you, you can write a list of things that were said to you that just did not help. Often bizarre phrases like,

"Life is like a football game. Sometimes you just get a bad bounce."

"At least you have other children."

"God must have needed another angel"

In the midst of grief's pain, people can be so desperate to comfort and make a situation positive that they say things to try and comfort, yet too frequently words meant to comfort can easily have the opposite effect. I love Amy Post's perspective in her essay following chapter two when she says that she learned to translate people's unhelpful or even hurtful comments into "I love you. I am here for you." Maybe those are the phrases we should start using intentionally instead of trying to find something positive to say.

In her insightful book *What Grieving People Wish You Knew* Nancy Guthrie points out that if you feel tempted to start a sentence with "Well, at least..." then it is probably better left unsaid. "'Well, at least he didn't suffer'; 'Well at least we know where she is'; or 'Well at least you still have your other children.' When we say such things, we think we're helping grieving people look on the bright side. We want to finish our conversation with them on a happy and hopeful note. But what they want are friends who are willing to sit with them in the darkness, feeling the weight of the loss with them. We think they need perspective. But what they need is time and freedom to lament their loss."[32]

Guthrie does go on to say that in a survey she did of people who had lost loved ones there were two things that people often *did* want to hear which were firstly "stories about the person who died and specific things she said or did that were meaningful and memorable" and secondly "to keep saying the name of the person who died."[33]

Instead of trying to make it better with your words, use your words to celebrate the person who has passed on. Talk about the unique way he or she lived life. Write out a favorite story or memory that you have. These words will be treasured because they are an intimate way of stepping into loss and honoring a life instead of trying to rush a griever into happier days.

When it comes to words of comfort, sharing scripture with those who are grieving can be helpful, although at times this practice can be equally harmful. If a verse is used to shut down conversation or make light of something complex, this can be damaging. Scripture, of course, holds our greatest hope; but when taken out of context and thrown at someone even verses of truth can come across as insensitive and unhelpful.

When it comes to sharing a verse don't force it. If, while you are reading scripture, a person's name comes to mind; it may be that you should share what you read with your friend and tell them that while reading it you thought of them. But, if the use of a verse is to try and tie a neat scriptural bow on a messy situation this is not a helpful approach.

Veentha Rendall puts it well in her article, "How to Discourage a Suffering Friend,"

"When I'm in agony, I don't want trite comments. When someone tells me to count my blessings; my plight could be worse; there are starving orphans in Africa who have a much harder situation, I want to scream. Of course, these things are all true. But at that moment, they feel irrelevant. Pat answers sound sermonizing. Saying that all things work together for good is absolutely true, but it feels hollow at a funeral. Besides, unasked for advice is criticism…When people minimize my struggle, it magnifies my pain."[34]

> If a verse is used to shut down conversation or make light of something complex, this can be damaging. Scripture, of course, holds our greatest hope; but when taken out of context and thrown at someone even verses of truth can come across as insensitive and unhelpful.

Let's commit to not magnifying someone's pain by being extra sensitive about the words we choose to say and sometimes even more importantly choose *not* to say to those in the midst of mourning.

But, there are times to speak. People surrounded by grief are often searching for words of hope and comfort. This is why words spoken at a funeral service or memorial can be especially moving. My husband was asked to preach at the funeral for our son's classmate. He spoke from 2 Corinthians chapter 1. Verses 3-5 Say "Blessed be the God and Father of our Lord Jesus Christ, the Father of mercies and God of all comfort, who comforts us in all our affliction, so that we may be able to comfort those who are in any affliction, with the comfort we ourselves are comforted by God. For as we share abundantly in Christ's sufferings, so through Christ we share abundantly in comfort too."

It was especially heartbreaking to hear the eulogy of a four year old. His favorite color was green. He loved drums and used to always want to help the musicians at church pack up the drum set after the service. He wanted to join the army when he grew up—unfulfilled dreams of a young, energetic boy. As his young aunt read the simple eulogy one of the other youth held the microphone for her. When her voice started to shake, he supportively put his hand around her shoulder giving her strength to finish her simple tribute. All his little classmates (including my five year-old and two year-old) stood with their teachers to sing a final song for their little friend. As those tiny voices sang Michael W. Smith's song "Friends" it made me think of how the Holy Spirit prays for us when we have no words. Romans 8:26 says, "Likewise the Spirit helps us in our weakness. For we do not know what to pray for as we ought, but the Spirit himself intercedes for us with groanings too deep for words." Songs and poetry often serve a similar purpose providing an outlet for expression when hearts are too heavy to speak.

As my husband concluded his time of sharing, he pointed out that this young death is an especially difficult reality to accept, particularly for the family. A life gone too soon—what can you say really? He encouraged us all not to avoid difficult situations like this but to, "be engaged. Do what you can to comfort. You can't do everything, but do what you can." Practical advice for all of us who know someone in the process of mourning. There is "a time to keep silent and a time to speak" (Ecclesiastes 3:7 NIV) says. May our words be words of genuine comfort spoken after much prayer and thought. May our willingness to be present be more abundant than a tendency to utter hollow clichés. May we allow time for the prompting of the Holy Spirit to guide our words sharing truth, but also sharing silence. May our words be not so much about making ourselves feel better and trying to explain away complex pain, but may they be gracious, full of love not condemning or trite platitudes.

"Gracious words are like a honeycomb, sweetness to the soul and health to the body." —Proverbs 16:24

I Love You Twice As Much

By Dr. Cristian Ile

IT'S BEEN TWENTY-FIVE years… twenty-five years since that cold, dark, heartbreaking- soul wrenching 5 am Monday morning, the Monday morning that would forever change me and my family; well, whatever was left of us without mom.

People say "time heals everything." I totally disagree; only those who haven't lost a loved one yet can believe in that tale. Only the eternal hope of being reunited with our loved ones can help alleviate the pain.

I had a very happy childhood. I used to love to play outside and run barefoot even across the rocks that were so prevalent in the sidewalks in Romania in the eighties. I loved soccer, and kids, eating the first cherries in May and drinking freshly squeezed grape juice from our own grapes. While the grape press was tantalizing my taste buds as it pressed on the grapes, I remember standing as a little boy in front of it with a glass and getting the very first drops of juice. Our family used to go on picnics, grill and enjoy mom's scrumptious cakes not only on the weekend, but also on Tuesday evenings. Yes, Tuesday evenings as well! Back then all the moms would normally bake on the weekend. My mom baked me a cake or some type of yummy dessert on Tuesdays as well. So I asked her, "Mom, why do you bake twice a week when every other mom only bakes once?" With a loving and warm smile, she gave me a chilling answer, even prophetic—"So that if one day I am gone you can remember that I loved you very much." Loved me she did! One of my aunts, mom's sister and best friend, told me years later that she had never witnessed a human being love another as much as my mom loved me. So to this day I remember warmly, yet with a chill down my spine, my mom's out of the ordinary love for me—the son she had hoped and prayed for many years similar to biblical Hannah.

My mom was my universe; when I was sad, she always found a way to encourage me. When I was angry, she and grandma looked for ways to help me work through my anger. When mom cooked, I was her helper. When mom baked, I was her taste tester. When she was tired and needed a back massage or a foot massage, I ever so gladly offered my services only to help reduce her weariness. We were hardly ever separated. We often rode the train to go visit my grandparents, and we would talk about all sorts of things during those long train rides. My mom was my best friend and my favorite chef and baker in the whole world. She was the one who could make it all better. She was the center of my world. If my childhood was happy and bright, it was because mom was the star at the center of my universe, ever emanating warmth, kindness, love and cakes.

There was, nonetheless, a dark shadow that loomed large in the background of my childhood. My grandma, my dad's mom, passed away when I was a one-year-old baby. I can't even remember her. Then, my eight to nine year old's world was confused as the doctor started to visit my other grandma, my mom's mom, who favored me out of her twenty or so grandkids, of that I am certain! She almost always sensed we were coming although we had no cell phone or phone. She somehow knew and would have my favorite meal cooking or just finished as we entered her house. My confused world turned to worry as grandma didn't seem to get out of bed much anymore, until one day grandma's eyes closed to never open again in this world. As a ten-year-old I left her funeral first; I couldn't hold back the tears anymore. Somehow, I sensed that my world was never going to be the same again without my "buna" (the Romanian word for grandparent which literally means good one). Not long after her, mom got sick. Then grandpa, then the other grandpa and somewhere in the middle a close aunt and an uncle. They all passed away before I turned eighteen. The pain is too much to internalize and carry even now as a grown man. I don't allow my mind to dwell on it; I never have. This was my coping mechanism. I would shut off and seal off the pain, death and loss as if locked away in a safe. This little child's grief safe got ever bigger—full beyond capacity. The door would often bust at the seams in spite of my best efforts to keep it under many locks by neglect, pretending it doesn't exist or that it never happened. I would change the topic or stop a sad movie such as *A Walk to Remember*. But there would be moments that took me off guard, and the thick door to my "non-existent" excruciating pain safe flung open with such power that I couldn't contain my tears for hours.

Even now, I am avoiding diving into the most cold, dark time in my life. I have to slowly circle around it and perhaps land but for a moment in that valley of sorrows where even the roses are of black, cold stones and the bird's songs cannot be heard. The silence is deafening as tears billow like a massive wave pushing against a dam which is often too weak to keep the tears from spilling over. How did my deeply wounded soul make this journey, alone? I often am in wonder.

A couple of years after buna Maria, my mom's mom, passed away; a little mole on my mom's skin started rapidly devolving into a monstrous cancer. At first, shock and unbelief; mom has cancer. Oh God, the year and a half medical journey was going to be more than any of us could bear! First unbelief; we were in shock at the initial results. Then, cautious hope that the 90s medicine could treat this. A desperate surgery followed, trying to eliminate the dark demon so unwilling to unclench its claws from mom's skin and body. Then, silence. Relief. Joy, ever so cold and crisp, unsure if it will last. The month-long deception gave us a small reprieve to enjoy our mom, the queen of our home, once again. We played volleyball and laughed with relief and cooked and baked and thanked God. Meanwhile, the dark and maddened cells went deeper, spread faster, and eventually reappeared wider than before. In no time we were at the hospital again. After a quick scan it was revealed that there was nothing else modern medicine could do. That felt like a polar-cold stalactite thrust through my heart that for a passing moment had warmed up again—that freezing, agonizing, unyielding, merciless master of pain stunned all of our hearts and left us agonizing in emotions too intense to handle like an erupting volcano that cannot be contained.

A new strategy was needed; mom and dad began a mad search for that one miraculous plant with healing powers. Eventually we found a herbalist family who promised miracles but never delivered. Prayer was tried throughout this time; churches and relatives prayed for mom, for us and with us. Then all these people forgot, ever so quickly, about those left behind. Almost all forgot, but the few who didn't, made the biggest difference in my life post-mom to this day. Two of mom's sisters, as well as my sister, would become my angels up until the time I met and married my own beautiful angel, Lindsey, my bride.

Once we realized that the too costly and terribly tasting herbal treatments were to no avail, we ceased trying any other treatment, except for prayer. The nefarious sickness was rapidly, and painfully, taking over more and more of mom's body. By now we were trying to contain our emotions and preserve our energy. Both were long gone; we were running on empty trying to look strong for mom as dad and a best girlfriend of mom's were cleaning her wounds and administering morphine daily to help alleviate the pain.

Somehow, during the process, when mom was still well enough; she wrote my sister a letter that would become our family's treasure, a warm touch of mom's heart and presence. She also totally repainted the entire house to help dad have one less worry once she was gone. It would be years before we would dare paint the house again.

Eventually, that agonizing Sunday night when only God knows what mom and dad told each other. Mom came to a final rest early on Monday morning. I remember, though I'd rather not, how dad woke me up to give me the news, stern as a statue that was crushed on the inside. We hugged briefly and rushed to separate rooms. At thirteen, all that grandma and mom taught me, although I was unaware, was helping me withstand the greatest test of my life and faith. I prayed, not to God but to the devil. It was a battle cry, my own, declaring eternal war on his evil plans that brought sin, death and destruction to mankind and as a result of it the untimely death of my mom at age forty-two. I prayed again and again and again. I wanted to scream to God from the top of my lungs as my mom's body lay in the open casket before me for three days. When her body was taken to the gravesite, I was comforted ever so slightly by the unusually large crowd who had come to honor mom and by my dad and sister walking alongside me.

The next four to five years would be void of prayer, void of talk, void of thought and void of daring to even say a word to God except for the occasional whyyyyyy? which would erupt from the depths of my heart. The little loved boy turned into an untimely matured man, trying to look fine on the outside. Then, one day, healing began to take place like a little plant sprouting from beneath a cracked glacier. At my aunt Ani's house, God graced upon me the realization that I did have a mom for almost fourteen years, something that many children never experienced. Yes, I am an orphan, but I had received so much love from my grandma and from my mom in those few short foundational years that their influence in my life would never leave me. God kept them in my life just long enough for them to pass onto me the key to healing and hope—a love for the Bible.

My ongoing healing process ensued with a thirst to read the Bible and to know the God of the Bible. Unaware of my need, I also turned my huge emotional void into a massive love for people. I so desperately needed friends and family and discovered that so many around me were also broken and lonely. I walked the grieving journey with some of them just long enough to keep them from becoming emotionally codependent on me. Ten years later I had more best friends than anyone else. These were deep, genuine friendships and each of them filled my emotional abyss at a critical time or another. Lastly, in my late twenties, a discerning pastor taught me the principles of the supernatural exchange. Simply put, I sometimes patched my grieving pain with food, anger or deep sorrow, instead of taking these dead-end roads, I learned to turn to God and ask Him to take my strong emotions leading to various negative outcomes and to replace them with healing, peace and the hope of eternity with mom. My cold Monday morning will one day turn to a glorious heavenly encounter with my amazing mom!

A Psalm for Reflection

Psalm 116

I love the LORD, for he heard my voice;
he heard my cry for mercy.
Because he turned his ear to me,
I will call on him as long as I live.
The cords of death entangled me,
the anguish of the grave came over me;
I was overcome by distress and sorrow.
Then I called on the name of the LORD
"LORD, save me!"
The Lord is gracious and righteous;
our God is full of compassion.
The LORD protects the unwary;
when I was brought low, he saved me.
Return to your rest, my soul,
for the LORD has been good to you.
For you, LORD, have delivered me from death,
my eyes from tears,
my feet from stumbling,
that I may walk before the LORD
in the land of the living.
I trusted in the LORD when I said,
"I am greatly afflicted";
in my alarm I said,
"Everyone is a liar."
What shall I return to the LORD
for all his goodness to me?
I will lift up the cup of salvation

*and call on the name of the LORD.
I will fulfill my vows to the LORD
in the presence of all his people.
Precious in the sight of the LORD
is the death of his faithful servants.
Truly I am your servant, LORD;
I serve you just as my mother did;
you have freed me from my chains.
I will sacrifice a thank offering to you
and call on the name of the LORD.
I will fulfill my vows to the LORD
in the presence of all his people,
in the courts of the house of the Lord
—in your midst, Jerusalem.
Praise the LORD (NIV).*

CHAPTER ELEVEN

It's Complicated

"Grief is so tricky that way. It doesn't really go away. We always carry it. It's kind of like having a backpack that can't be taken off. Sometimes it is so light I almost forget I have it on, I can even pull out a little memory with a smile... and other times, like holidays or even when a certain song comes on... it feels like someone has filled it with rocks. It's so heavy I don't understand how I can move forward."

–Hannah Dearth

There were two deaths within our church family this week. Since we are in the midst of Covid and our city is in partial lockdown with a nightly curfew, haus krais are being discouraged. My heart goes out to the families all over the world who have lost loved ones and are not even able to follow the normal cultural practices of grieving due to the state that the world is currently in. My heart hurts for families who have had to have a tiny funeral in keeping with Covid regulations. My heart hurts for loved ones who have not even been able to travel to the funeral of a family member due to travel restrictions. Sometimes grief is added on top of grief.

Facing the death of a loved one is never easy and yet there are times when grief is even more complex due to the surrounding circumstance. This can especially be the case when the death was sudden or unexpected, when the person's death was surrounded by traumatic circumstances like a murder, a car accident or suicide. Sometimes there is no body for a proper burial or circumstances make it impossible to attend the funeral and these things can be especially difficult for finding a sense of closure.

My maternal grandfather passed away while my husband and I were in Australia en route to come to Papua New Guinea. This made attending his funeral difficult as we had just left the US weeks before. He passed away in April, but I found that I did not actually process his death until December of that year. It was our first Christmas in PNG, just our second Christmas as a married couple; and out of nowhere I felt so homesick. As someone who has travelled a lot, I do not actually find myself feeling home sick often. I love my family and treasure times with them, but it is not often that the deep pain of being separated by oceans really hits me. That hot, sticky Christmas, it hit me—and it hit me hard. I remember crying and not even being sure why I was crying. Later it dawned on me that part of the reason I was feeling so homesick was that we would often spend Christmas in sandy Florida where my grandparents lived. I finally realized that part of my homesickness was me finally coming to terms with the fact that my grandpa was no longer on this earth and a Christmas at his house would never happen again like they had for so many years. This realization has helped me be more intentional about celebrating future Christmases knowing that these extra emotions are now attached to Christmas. For me, Christmas has now become a natural time when I remember my grandpa just like I think about my grandma when I drink lemonade out of the glass tumbler of hers that I kept with the lightly etched scene of Victorian picnickers enjoying a summer day.

We mourn people, memories and simpler times and when we are far away physically; it can be even harder to go through that process. When my aunt, passed away earlier this year, I once again found myself oceans away from family when I wanted to be close. With a nursing baby whose passport was stuck in red tape, I could not easily fly back to the US. So I did what I could. I wrote a short piece in memory of my aunt that my cousins later asked my sister to read at her memorial service. Circumstances made it difficult for me to be there but at least through thoughts and words I was able to process some of my own grief and also celebrate my aunt and the life that she lived even if it was from a far.

Of course there is never an ideal time to lose a loved one, but if you do find yourself in especially challenging circumstances give yourself extra grace as you mourn. You may need to get a bit more creative with how you remember your loved one. It may take months for the loss to really sink in. You might find yourself mourning the loss of a loved one and also mourning the fact that you were unable to be present with family or that circumstances were much different then you would have preferred.

Grief is not a straight path. It can feel more like a twisted maze. There are many hills and valleys, roundabouts and even dead ends along the way. It would be nice to work through five easy steps and be on your way, but that is just not the reality of how grief actually works. The pain sticks—it sticks to every part of your being and moving forward means learning to move with a new companion called pain.

As a twin, it took me years to finally realize why my birthday was often such an emotional day. I finally connected the mental dots on my 16th birthday when after an especially beautiful day full of friends and sweet memories, I once again found myself crying in bed after the lights were out. "Why, I thought, "after such a wonderful day am I crying?" and then it hit me the subconscious thought that it was my twin sister Allison's birthday as well. I was not thinking about it, and yet somehow I was. This is part of what can make grief so complicated. Much of it can be subconscious. The ways it affects you and the ways that you do not even realize that it is affecting you can take years to even understand. If anything, grief is complicated.

> Grief is not a straight path. It can feel more like a twisted maze. There are many hills and valleys, roundabouts and even dead ends along the way. It would be nice to work through five easy steps and be on your way, but that is just not the reality of how grief actually works. The pain sticks—it sticks to every part of your being and moving forward means learning to move with a new companion called pain.

Grief can be complicated as well in that just as people love differently, people also grieve differently. Maybe there should be a study on identifying the five (or possibly more) languages of grief expression just as there have been studies identifying different love languages. When processing grief, some people want to talk constantly or post frequently about the person that they lost. Others barely mention or acknowledge the loss. It is important to make space for both. Pushing back or not dealing with emotions is not healthy, but some people need less time to verbally process then others or do not find frequently discussing their loss necessary.

While all grief is complicated, it is good to give extra space to process when the loss of a loved one was not a "typical" death. Maybe the person died very suddenly or was very young. Maybe the relationship with the person who passed on was a strained one. Maybe, as mentioned, the person died while you were away, or severe trauma surrounded their death. Maybe there is plaguing guilt that makes it hard to accept what happened. Take time and pray through these extra complicated factors realizing that yes, this is hard or not the "norm." Give yourself space and time to really examine what extra factors are playing a part in this wound as understanding those factors will help bring healing.

Taking time to fully understand a grief wound is vital as it will affect many other areas of your life. How deep is it? Are there layers to your grief? If so, take time to really come to terms with what those layers are. My best friend faced a devastating miscarriage when she lost her daughter. She has three amazing boys, but has always dreamed of a daughter. For health reasons she has been advised not to get pregnant again. With her loss she not only lost a child, but she also lost a much longed for dream of having a little girl. Again, grief layered upon grief needing extra time and energy to work through.

Permission to Mourn

The complications of losing a loved one can start even before a loved one leaves this earth. This morning I got an email from my cousin. Her dad recently returned from doing ministry in Africa to undergo treatment for colon cancer. It was not an easy email to read. The cancer has spread more extensively than first believed, making surgery no longer an option unless this aggressive and rare cancer reacts well to the chemo treatments, which he will start tomorrow. Generally patients with this rare form of cancer and at this stage are given six months to a year to live. My other cousins are in the process of travelling to be with their dad during this very difficult time. The whole family is praying God's will even to the point that my uncle said he is, "extremely excited to see His heavenly father." Bringing to mind the verse from Philippians 1:21 "For me to live is Christ, and to die is gain." My uncle (technically my mom's cousin but I have always called him uncle) spent the majority of his life as a missionary pilot dedicated to serving others and bringing people to a saving knowledge of Christ and His love. His life has been a life of service and while he is ready to meet his Savoir, it is still hard for those of us left behind. He is still in his sixties and was still actively serving on the field. He is a man who has been such a blessing to so many, and it will not be easy at all to say goodbye once his time on earth finishes whether that be within this next year or forty years from now.

And yet (what a beautiful phrase) and yet there is always hope even in the most complicated grief. As one processes through grief that feels more complicated than the typical grief there is always hope in the knowledge that God is still God, so once again we choose to grieve while clinging to hope. The God that we serve has the ability to redeem even the deepest hurts no matter how layered or complex. In His timing and in His unique way He makes all things beautiful in His time. He is the great restorer, the healer, the redeemer, the beginning and the end. He writes the end of the story and that end is a glorious one even if it means loved ones entering heaven before we were ready to let them go.

> "Precious in the sight of the LORD is the death of his saints."
> —Psalm 116:15 (KJV)

Trigger Warning

By Kristen Flores

FOR A TIME, I wished the Oscars included a trigger warning. No, it wasn't because of the long winded speeches or sometimes subpar celebrity hosts. I used to love the entire ceremony, long speeches and all. But this changed during a 2015 Oscar party when, in between bites of *hor d'oeuvres* and snippets of awards commentary, I glanced at my phone during a commercial break to see the subject line "Sad News" in my inbox.

The sender was a friend from college, which had been over a decade earlier at that point, and I assumed that Sarah's Mom had lost her battle with cancer after many years. But maybe it's one of her kids, I thought anxiously as I instinctively opened the email. What I read was not something I ever would have been prepared for: Judy, the wife of my campus minister and my own mentor/friend/spiritual mother, had died that morning. While I immediately suspected a freak accident or undiagnosed terminal illness, I was shocked by the truth revealed as I kept reading: Judy had died by her own hand. At the time, I had no context for such a death. I had always been at least one step removed from someone who had committed suicide. The thought that someone who trusted Jesus during her life could also put an end to that very same life sent my mind into a tailspin.

I had some idea that Judy had wrestled with her mental health over the years from the time we spent in geographic proximity, but these acknowledgments were presented with very superficial details such as, "years ago, I experienced a rough period of postpartum depression" or "My anxiety is bad right now." As a teenager/twenty-something who had personally only struggled with minor bouts of clinical depression and not a single suicidal thought that I could remember, I simply could not fathom the deep wounds hiding behind Judy's vague descriptions. In my ignorance and naiveté, I found myself in pure shock that this woman, I admired so deeply, could not only experience such a valley but would go as far as to succumb completely to such a tragic temptation.

That infamous Oscar night, I called my husband to come pick me up. I needed to leave the party but didn't trust myself to drive home in my emotional state. "I have bad news," I got out before dissolving into sobs then finally continuing, "Judy died. She killed herself."

Later that night, my bewildered husband gently critiqued my presentation because, in the moment when I had paused before delivering the news, he had thought my sobs meant that one of our parents must have died. I'm not sure if it was then or sometime later, but I held my hands about a foot apart and, shaking one hand and then the other, explained, "For you, there's family… and then there's friends." Moving my "friend" hand an inch or two away from my "family" hand, I continued, "For me, Judy was here."

The day after Judy died, I decided to go to work. I thought the distraction would be a better alternative to staying home alone stuck in my head all day and that the work I did would actually honor her memory. Judy had counseled me in living as a Christian through my entire college career and for the 5ish years I had stayed in that area after graduating (I had spent one of those years in Uganda, and during that time Judy and her kids had written me a number of encouraging letters). I coordinated a tutoring program, facilitating almost 100 tutoring/mentoring relationships between volunteers and kids from mostly refugee backgrounds; being present for them seemed a testament to my relationship with Judy.

When I arrived home, my husband innocently and far too casually asked, "How was your day?"

I barked, "You know, your usual day-after-your-friend-commits-suicide kind of day." At some point that week, I realized that my expectation for my husband-of-just-over-a-year to share in my grief in a way that viscerally matched my own was unreasonable. I had to come to terms with the fact that while Judy played such a vital role in my life, this was mostly before I had met my husband. For him, Judy was one of a handful of nice middle-aged churchwomen he had met only a few times when we made the 900+ mile trek to the East Coast.

While he grew in how he comforted me in the days and weeks to come, I also expanded my circle of support, turning mostly to friends from college who also felt Judy's loss as deeply as I had, talking with them on the phone and eventually mourning together in person the following week thanks to a friend who graciously bought me a plane ticket "home."

Judy's death rattled me to the core. My head would literally start to hurt as I thought about the ramifications of her suicide. The fact that the blood of Jesus could cover such an act disturbed me as much as it reassured me. But why should anyone stick around when life gets tough if you just get to be with Jesus?

And what did it mean for our relationship that I hadn't realized Judy suffered so significantly? Sure we were half a country away and talked sporadically at that point, but what did it mean that seemingly none of her friends had noticed either? Judy was known for asking probing questions that penetrated the heart. Had no one thought to ask her these same questions? Or was it that Judy could sit with the vulnerable without ever being truly vulnerable herself? I wondered if Judy had felt as though she could give help, guidance, support and encouragement but not receive it.

For a long time, I was angry with her and felt betrayed by her. Often she would appear in my dreams, and I would coldly say to her, "Aren't you supposed to be dead? Why are you here?"

I was uncomfortable with how Judy's death seemed to complicate things. It became easier to let Judy's tragic death overshadow any good I had gleaned from her in life because to do otherwise made for a messy narrative and more pain (I subconsciously seemed to calculate that the less valuable a friend she was, the less it hurt to lose her). As I reflected on our relationship, I began to focus on the handful of times she had let me down instead in order to escape these tensions:

- The saint who had pointed me to Christ during my low times had lost sight of Him when faced with her own
- The woman who seemingly had the capacity for giving so much life could also bring about her own unfortunate death

I also began to worry that maybe I would meet the same end. I had followed Judy's example in so many other ways in my life, I figured, I might follow her in death too. By God's grace, I had never before thought about taking my own life, but suddenly it seemed possible. Occasionally a thought would work its way into my mind: "What if you just ended everything?"

The subject of suicide became a source of morbid curiosity. I felt desperate to understand it and began to read as much as I could as though any amount of research could help me grasp why Judy –or anyone –decided to end his or her life. And anytime I stumbled on (or recalled) an ambiguous obituary, I obsessed over digging for details because I was certain that no spoken cause of death often meant suicide, and I felt it absolutely necessary to know if that was the case.

It has taken years, but God has done redemptive work in my heart and mind. I can now think of Oscar Night without feeling a sense of dread in the pit of my stomach or experiencing sweaty palms or heart palpitations. I'm a sucker for symbolism and story lines, yet I've somehow never stopped to think about what it means to have been watching that ceremony when I learned of Judy's death.

At the end of Oscar night, the Academy has presented the best of the best: the winners are clear. There is the Best Actress, Best Director, Best Film, and so on. The winners, regardless of the lives they live off screen or the characters they depict on screen, are dressed glamorously, their speeches gushing with gratitude, their faces glowing and their statues gleaming.

No matter the stories behind the Oscar performances, the overall outcome is always the same on Oscar Night. When I thought of Judy, I wanted her to be a polished performer grasping a golden Oscar statue and not a raw example of real life lived off screen. Thanks to the healing hand of the Lord through a multitude of good counselors and other experiences of grace, I can finally think of Judy without a ragged restlessness taking over my brain. I recognize that I will never know precisely why she thought the world would be better without her or why God didn't allow her to fail in pulling the trigger on that fateful February day… and I can accept that it is not my place to know. Instead of highlighting Judy's flaws and staying primarily angry with her, I've come to see Judy in her humanity and view her with a growing compassion and grace. She must have been in so much pain…

Judy was so good at supporting me through issues with my health and initial experiences with infertility. She often made a point to call me right after an appointment and prayed over the brokenness in my body. Two and half years after her death, after three years of trying to conceive, I finally had my first positive pregnancy test. It was late July and just days before what would have been Judy's birthday. I was filled with an overwhelming sadness that I couldn't call to share the news. Judy adored babies. In fact, she had been a doula and had helped to bring many babies to life.

The reality that Judy could literally bring others to life while also putting an end to her own no longer makes me angry with her, but it does make me both miss and mourn for her. In 2019, both of my parents died followed by my mother-in-law in 2020, and while none of those deaths were suicides, they each came with their own set of complications and confusing details. While most people, approximately 85% of Americans, don't directly die by their own hand, we all make choices that indirectly lead to death on a daily basis (choosing to eat an unhealthy diet, deciding to drive while distracted, giving in to sin of any kind). Death, however it comes, is not the way it is supposed to be an indicative of a world blemished by that very first bite of forbidden fruit.

Six years later, I still wonder about the seemingly healthy 30-year-olds who suddenly die, but I've mostly stopped the compulsive Internet dives into their personal lives to confirm my suspicions. I will probably always wince when I see some bored or frustrated individual pointing a finger in the form of the gun at their temple or I overhear someone casually remark, "I would just kill myself if my husband was like that." But, finally, at the age of thirty-nine, I am also coming to terms with the fact that just as life is messy and doesn't come with clear answers, so often death is just as messy and unclear.

A Psalm for Reflection

Psalm 42

As the deer longs for streams of water,
so I long for you, O God.
I thirst for God, the living God.
When can I go and stand before him?
Day and night I have only tears for food,
while my enemies continually taunt me, saying,
"Where is this God of yours?"
My heart is breaking
as I remember how it used to be:
I walked among the crowds of worshipers,
leading a great procession to the house of God,
singing for joy and giving thanks
amid the sound of a great celebration!
Why am I discouraged?
Why is my heart so sad?
I will put my hope in God!
I will praise him again—
my Savior and my God!
Now I am deeply discouraged,
but I will remember you—
even from distant Mount Hermon, the source of the Jordan,
from the land of Mount Mizar.
I hear the tumult of the raging seas
as your waves and surging tides sweep over me.
But each day the Lord pours his unfailing love upon me,
and through each night I sing his songs,
praying to God who gives me life.

*"O God my rock," I cry,
"Why have you forgotten me?
Why must I wander around in grief,
oppressed by my enemies?"
Their taunts break my bones.
They scoff, "Where is this God of yours?"
Why am I discouraged?
Why is my heart so sad?
I will put my hope in God!
I will praise him again—
my Savior and my God! (NLT)*

CHAPTER TWELVE

Surviving the Landmines

> *"We tend to stay away from mourning and dancing: too afraid to cry, too shy to dance... we become narrow-minded complainers, avoiding pain and also true human joy... While we live in a world subject to the evil one, we belong to God. Let us mourn, let us dance."*
>
> —Henri J. M. Nouwen

I broke down and cried during a health and wellness class my senior year of college. Not an ideal place to start crying, I know; but then again where is? It had been such a normal day. I had already finished three classes and this was my last class before I left to tutor. Everything was going well until some of my classmates stood up to present their class project —the process of grieving. Instantly, my palms got sweaty. I could feel my heart beating faster. I began giving myself a mental pep talk knowing that this had the potential to be a very painful presentation.

Part of me was glad that in a class on wellness a group had picked this difficult topic. The other part of me dreaded the next forty-five minutes. The group started out by having people stand to show the percent of the class who had lost a close relative or friend.

Permission to Mourn

As I stood and looked around, it was comforting, in a sad way, to see around two-thirds of the room standing.

The lecture was informative. One student covered the stages of grief and talked about how her grandfather had recently passed away. The next person who spoke was a Resident Assistant who had recently had a girl on her dorm floor experience the death of a parent. She shared some tips for dealing with friends who had lost a loved one and also talked about the importance of counseling. The last student presenting simply told her story, and that's when I started to lose it.

She was eight when her brother was killed while serving in the Israeli army, the same age I had been when my twin sister died suddenly. Her very words made my heart ache because they mirrored parts of my own story, and yet I was surprised that she was able to tell it with a calm voice and even with a slight smile.

I held it together until it was time for questions. I wanted to ask how to deal with those unexpected landmines of grief that just hit you out of nowhere. Memories and emotions triggered by something simple and coming, of course, at the most inconvenient times. I thought I could do it without crying in front of the entire class, but as I asked the question, unwelcome tears welled up in my eyes. Today had turned into one of those landmine days.

What do you do when unwanted tears come, when a song on the radio throws you back into more emotion then you feel able to process? What do you do when you think things are going well and then something as simple as the smell of cologne leaves you weeping uncontrollable?

One thing you can always do is just breathe—a short breath in and a long breath out. This simple act can help physically calm the body, something that can help give you time to process. Other times you might just need to have a good cry. Do not always feel that you have to fight the emotional urge to cry. Find a safe space or a safe person to be with if you can. Give yourself permission to sit, for a moment, with the pain and the hurt instead of pushing it back. A simple breath prayer can also help to refocus and calm the heart or take a minute to meditate on a promise from scripture. Find a passage that speaks comfort and when grief threatens to leave you feeling hopeless, center yourself back on hope.

Just this week while scrolling Facebook I was reminded of how easy it can be for pain to be triggered. "He didn't watch rugby for the longest time." One friend posted about how her dad lost interest in one of his favorite pastimes after one of his daughters passed away. It used to be a passion that the two of them enjoyed together. Now it had become a trigger, reminding him of the pain of loss. "It's not easy to single parent," another friend wrote. His wife passed away from cancer earlier this year and even though his children are now grown, some even with children of their own, he misses his wife's steady advice and the unique role that she played as they loved their grown children together.

I was reading a library book from the Redwall series when I found out that the wife of my dad's best friend and two of their children had been brutally murdered during a tribal conflict in their home in Congo. It was a book from one of my favorite series, at the time, where mice and other woodland creatures bravely defended their Abby home from invaders. I returned the book unread and never read another one from that series. Every time I picked it up to read it, I felt the emotions flooding back—too much pain, too much violence, too much sadness was now linked to a story I once enjoyed.

When those landmine moments hit. Do not give in to the temptation to turn away from offers of comfort. Not everyone around you will be at a place where they can offer comfort or even begin to understand what you are going through, but some will. Resist the temptation to completely pull away from those who genuinely do want to help.

After that health and wellness class I mentioned in the introduction to this chapter, one of my fellow students made an effort to take the time to talk with me, ask questions, and just listen. I had met her briefly before, but did not know her well. In spite of that, she took the time to engage and offer comfort which meant so much. She had not personally experienced what I had in terms of the sudden loss of a sibling, but she is no stranger to suffering as she faces the daily battle of facing life with cystic fibrosis.[35] Because of her own struggles, she is quick to relate to others experiencing pain, and has a special gift of encouragement. The student from Israel, who had shared her story in class, also reached out to me offering just to get together and talk. So we made time to do just that. Sitting overlooking the campus plaza with drinks from JOE's in our hands we shared pieces of our stories with each other and again that time of mutual sharing brought comfort.

Those landmine days will often come at inconvenient times, instead of brushing off those moments, try and see it as a time to do a heart check. Give yourself permission to mourn. Loss is still loss whether it happened five years ago or fifty years ago. For some people, taking time out to journal or write a letter to your loved one telling them how you still miss them can help. Not that it completely takes the pain away, but it allows the heart and mind time to process. Talk to a friend or a family member. Go for a walk. Grab a coffee. Write down a memory (funny or serious). Create something. Read the Psalms. Go for a run. Listen to a comforting song. Start a scrapbook of favorite photos. Find a restful or safe space and just allow yourself time to sit with your grief.

When those landmine days hit, use it as a time to reflect. See it as a signal that your mind and body need to release emotion. Do not run from that or brush it off. Take time to think about your loved one or do something that helps you feel close to them. One of my friends will often bake cinnamon rolls in memory of her mom because that is something that helps her feel connected to sweet memories. Another friend will stop off at a playground and take time out to swing because that is something that she and her mom used to do—swing and talk. When I lived closer, she would sometimes pick me up, and we would go and swing together. Now she takes her son with her when she feels that pull to swing.

> When those landmine days hit, use it as a time to reflect. See it as a signal that your mind and body need to release emotion. Do not run from that or brush it off. Take time to think about your loved one or do something that helps you feel close to them.

Permission to Mourn

Some landmine moments are easier to plan for—a wedding, an anniversary, your loved ones' birthday, the anniversary of their death, mother's day, father's day, the birth of a child. As beautiful as some of these moments can be, the longing that you wish your loved one was there with you can be a common time when joy and grief mingle. It can help to be as proactive as possible in those moments. Do not just hope that you will not be overcome with sadness at some point, instead try and think of ways to honor the memory of the person you are grieving during those special times. Maybe pick out an outfit for your new baby that you think your loved one would have liked to have given them. With a wedding without a loved one, whether that be a parent or a grandparent, sibling or close friend, try and brainstorm some ways to honor the person's memory during the ceremony. Something as simple as lighting a candle in their memory or including a picture, taking a moment to mention how their presence is missed or maybe wearing a piece of jewelry that reminds you of them. It can be something public or something completely personal that only you will know the significance of—a reminder that even though they are no longer on the earth, the person is still very much in your thoughts.

Questions, often asked by well meaning strangers, can also explode a landmine of emotion. "How many children do you have? How many siblings do you have?" "What do your parents do?" Questions that used to have easy straightforward answers can now bite with pain. This can especially be the case when one has faced the loss of miscarriage. A friend of mine told me that she dreaded going to the grocery store after one of her miscarriages because of running into well meaning friends who would ask how the baby was doing or how she was feeling. Questions which were too much to handle emotionally while in the middle of the aisles of Walmart. During those first few weeks of loss, she would intentionally go shopping with a friend or family member who could act as a shield or a bit of a buffer. If questions became too much to answer (whether well meaning questions or just nosey ones) the support person could then step in and take over answering the questions or simply steer the conversation in a different direction. Some people choose to drive to a completely different town to do errands just to avoid some of those painful interactions especially during the initial months when a simple greeting of, "how are you doing?" can feel like too much to answer.

I know another lady who would only do her shopping at 2 am after her husband passed away, again to avoid unwelcome questions. While it can be good to have some of these strategies in place, especially during the initial months of grief when coping and survival mode are often a way of life, avoidance should be a temporary solution. If, after a prolonged period of time, you are still choosing to drive out of your way to run simple errands or stop attending all functions where you will see people you know, this can be a sign that your heart and emotions need some more focused healing. You do not want to prematurely expose a gaping wound to harsh elements, but with time and intentionally sitting in lament, wounds can heal to a point that not every conversation is as painful as it initially was.

One way to learn how to navigate conversations so that they become less painful is to take some time to prepare how you might want to answer them. Sometimes a short simple answer is best. Not everyone needs, or deserves, to know your full story. When someone I just met asks me how many siblings I have, my answer often varies. Often I will say, "two brothers and a sister" and just leave it as that. Time, emotion and the particular setting often make this the best answer. If the person is someone that I can see developing a further relationship with; or if I think that sharing some of my story could help the person who asked, then I might include in my answer that I also have a twin sister who passed away when I was eight. Some people may connect well with this information, others might find it very uncomfortable, so when I share, I share with an open mind and then let the conversation continue or stop as it will.

Emotional landmines will hit. They hurt. They are unexpected, but they do not have to cripple you for the rest of the day, although some days that might happen and that is ok too! Focus on learning how to process when that happens. Focus on what provides comfort. Remember that you are not alone in these feelings and that deep grief is often the result of deep love. Just as it is good to love; it is good to grieve even when that grief feels like you walked into an emotional landmine.

"The hearts of the people cry out to the Lord. You walls of Daughter Zion, let your tears flow like a river day and night."
—Lamentations 2:18 (NIV)

The Sunshine of Life

By Heather Holdsworth

I WAS HUMMING a tune in the vitamin aisle when the text came in. Why do we remember the details? The fizzy tablets in my hand, the cart of food, the parking space. Words on the phone were distorted by poor reception and disbelief. The few that reached came tumbling in at the turn onto Broughton Road, 'tumour … they say there's nothing they can do.' There must be some mistake. We were having coffee on Monday at 8 pm. It was in the calendar.

We collect people. There are the honoured ones who live on our mantelpieces like so many shiny trophies. We know them through their resumes and they, us, by our eagerness to please. There are ones we keep in our pockets. Instafacetube folk who garnish our endeavours with grins but don't remember which sibling had the accident or how hope fades when we can't afford gas.

Then there is another category. She'd given me a book with the definition on the cover, *Friends are the Sunshine of Life*. We'd known each other since Mrs Brydon's form class. We'd cried, prayed and belly-laughed our way through the hubbub of years. On the day of Dad's funeral she'd taken a 30-minute taxi during her lunch break for three minutes and a hug outside the church. A few months later, she did the same for my Mum's funeral. We'd picked each other up on dark days and sunny ones, feasting on Bible chunks and finding fullness in God's presence.

The last year had been particularly challenging. We'd leaned hard on the Holy One as we stepped into unknown territory. She, from independence to adopting a vulnerable five year old: and I, from a dream ministry job that lay in fractured pieces. As we set ourselves to seek Him, weakness was flecked with courage; and hope grew.

But this? This couldn't be the plan. Surely there'd be a cure, a joyous victory, a story to tell. Besides, I'd never even been in a hospice room. We were in our 40s for goodness sake— it was time to live life to the edges! Yet in those three irrational bedside months, twice I left my friend's side to bury younger friends. Everything felt upside down.

Days melted away with mobility and memory. There was wrestling, praying and so much singing as we met Him, undone, with all the grit we could muster. One afternoon she looked up, her brow furrowed, "I think I'm part of your healing."

I stopped. Nodded. "I think you are, and I think I might be part of yours."

"Yes. I think you're right." We smiled grateful, watery smiles. With each day's losses, realization dawned, Sheonagh was waiting for Jesus' embrace. This wasn't going away.

Late one night three weeks before the end, she squeezed my hand and closed her eyes. *"God, I pray that my dear and lovely friend (names no longer worked) would be very kind with you when this is all over."* She stumbled over the words, confused. *"Is that what I mean, God? Yes. Yes, I believe it is. I pray that she would be very kind with you."* Kind.

We chose readings and songs. Then after days of quiet, she left us. Hundreds gathered to remember. There were flowers, good cake and a heart-stopping song "Bow the Knee."

"I pray that she will be kind with You." The words wouldn't let me go. Isn't kindness reserved for Heaven? A shiny future far from this wounding where hurt is banished and Jesus makes us strong?

Days passed, then weeks. We were in France enjoying the holidays when dawn rose on 2019. Morning laughter skipped upstairs as my phone lit up with New Year joy. Messages flew overhead like so many fireworks bursting the dark, but there was an empty patch of sky, and loss again smashed into my chest. Spent, I reached for my Bible, wondering where the year's readings would start.

Psalm 65 in all its generosity flooded the room, but it opened with a baffling phrase. "Praise waits for you, our God, in Zion" (NIV). Now "praise" made sense, that exuberant releasing joy, but why would it wait? Was it in storage; held in some celestial silo, waiting for heaven till we could applaud? Why the time lag, the gratitude gap; surely we could bring praise's freedom to this side of the divide?

But how?

It was within my reach in that upper room. I was being invited to more than mantlepiece trophy meetings; beyond an Instafacetube connection where I bedecked His achievements with the occasional grin. His welcome was to the sunshine of friendship built on the bravest trust. Trust. Trust that He had us, hadn't made some mistake, that He'd lived through what happened, that He knew the way home. Here lay kindness and the relief of praise.

"Go out into the darkness and put your hand into the hand of God. That shall be to you better than light and safer than a known way." —Minnie Louise Haskins

A Psalm for Reflection

Psalm 77

I cry aloud to God,
aloud to God, and he will hear me.
In the day of my trouble I seek the Lord;
in the night my hand is stretched out without wearying;
my soul refuses to be comforted.
When I remember God, I moan;
when I meditate, my spirit faints. Selah
You hold my eyelids open;
I am so troubled that I cannot speak.
I consider the days of old,
the years long ago.
I said, "Let me remember my song in the night;
let me meditate in my heart."
Then my spirit made a diligent search:
"Will the Lord spurn forever,
and never again be favorable?
Has his steadfast love forever ceased?
Are his promises at an end for all time?
Has God forgotten to be gracious?
Has he in anger shut up his compassion?" Selah

Then I said, "I will appeal to this,
to the years of the right hand of the Most High."
I will remember the deeds of the LORD;
yes, I will remember your wonders of old.
I will ponder all your work,
and meditate on your mighty deeds.

Your way, O God, is holy.
What god is great like our God?
You are the God who works wonders;
you have made known your might among the peoples.
You with your arm redeemed your people,
the children of Jacob and Joseph. Selah

When the waters saw you, O God,
when the waters saw you, they were afraid;
indeed, the deep trembled.
The clouds poured out water;
the skies gave forth thunder;
your arrows flashed on every side.
The crash of your thunder was in the whirlwind;
your lightnings lighted up the world;
the earth trembled and shook.
Your way was through the sea,
your path through the great waters;
yet your footprints were unseen.
You led your people like a flock
by the hand of Moses and Aaron.

CHAPTER THIRTEEN

Learning To Live Again

"One of the fastest paths to healing your hurt is to help someone else even while you are still hurting."

–Dr. Tony Evans

Last year while doing a retreat through Velvet Ashes, participants were encouraged to take out time to pray and ask God for a word, an identity in a way, to just listen in prayer for what God was saying, how He saw you. So, in the limited time that I had between nursing a three-month-old and pacing back and forth in hopes that she would sleep, the word that came to my mind was—healed. At the time I took it as physical healing I was dead in the middle of some of the worst physical pain I had ever experienced when a bout of mastitis turned into an abscess that eventually burst and took months and months to heal. I was in a rural village at the time that the abscess developed traveling on bumpy roads with very limited medical care, and I ended up having to dress a deep wound on my own (don't worry I will spare you the not so pleasant details). When a second abscess formed I was back in the city where my wonderful friend, who has had special training in wound care, took care of me. The second abscess healed quickly and without leaving a deep scar like the first abscess had done.

I learned a lot about wounds and how they heal during that excruciatingly painful experience. Some things I learned the hard way like, yes, it is better to make an incision and squeeze out the infection as painful as that is instead of letting it build up to the point of the infection bursting on its own. I learned that healing can take a long time, but as a wound heals not every day is as painful as when the wound first came to be. I learned that rest is vital. I learned that sometimes when a wound is particularly deep it has to be packed temporarily with sterile gauze so that it heals completely from the bottom up, not just new skin growing over a wound that is still there. I learned that healing is often much quicker and much less painful when getting care from a knowledgeable professional. I learned that if you are not extremely careful reinfection can happen. I learned that healing often happens much faster when the pain is reduced as much as is possible through medication and rest. I learned that some very painful and deep wounds will leave a permanent scar, but healing is still possible even though it alters you.

Healing is an active process that takes effort. Yes, it can be a painful process, but the pain is worth it as healing begins to take place. When I received that word *healed* during that time of prayer and retreat I saw it as a hope for physical healing, but as the year went on, God revealed to me that it was actually a two-part promise of physical healing and also emotional healing. That year I ended up having several needed conversations that I had been avoiding. Conversations while painful at times, brought needed emotional healing and a greater sense of peace.

Healing, what does it mean to heal after a loss that cuts deeply? Is it even truly possible? How do you live when a piece of you may not even want to live anymore without a person who meant so much? Giving yourself permission to mourn is so important as this can allow for the healing process to begin. You cannot just slap a Band-Aid on a deep wound. A Band-Aid may make the wound appear alright on the outside, but if the wound is not healing internally, it is not healing. Healing takes time and a lot of intentional, daily care to heal. It is equally important that someone in grief gives themselves permission to heal. Healing, learning to move forward again in life, is a choice and an active process. Life likely will not look the same as it did before loss. Scars will still likely be present; but, life, even a life of joy, is possible through Christ the one who heals all our afflictions and binds up all of our wounds.

I vividly remember the day my twin sister died, playing with our fuzzy black puppies with my friend Audrey. At one point I even remember laughing as we dressed the puppies in leaf coats and flower hats. Then, even as an eight-year-old, I caught myself. How can I be laughing right now? My world was just turned upside down. I think for children play can be a way of processing, a way of letting your mind release, in a sense, as it works to find a new normal. It is natural and normal to continue doing things that you love—it's even healthy to do so. The pain does not automatically go away. But, when you are able to, laughter truly can be a medicine that helps you move forward. Do not push those feelings of laughter or joy away, instead gratefully receive their healing presence. Allow recovery to happen as slow as it may be.

As a new normal is forming, know that laughter and tears will often be mixed. As kids we often enjoyed putting on little skits for our parents, usually a funny rendition of nursery rhyme acted out with simple costumes and props or no costumes at all. I remember shortly after my sister died doing one of our little skits for my mom. As she watched and smiled, tears also started to flow as she was painfully reminded that one of the little actors in our production would no longer be able to join us. To this day I still feel a pain in my heart whenever I hear the nursery rhyme. "Sing a Song of Six Pence," because that was the last rhyme Allison acted out before she left us. Yes, life continues, but it is not the same. And still it is so important to actively seek how to live again especially as time begins to pass.

One way to help with this process is to try and acknowledge, try and anticipate what things might be particularly painful as you process forward in life and specifically pray for comfort in these situations. The first Christmas without your cousin, the due date of the child you were never able to hold, the graduation that will not be witnessed by your grandfather who was your greatest cheerleader. These are all times to prepare for as life moves forward, which it will, whether you plan for it to or not. Give yourself extra grace on these days, but continue to live and celebrate life as I am sure your loved one would want you to do even if they are no longer able to be physically present with you.

Ultimately healing and the ability to move forward in life again is possible because of the Great Healer. Rest in this and know that it can take time to even do simple things again, but that does not mean that life will always be as pungently painful as it is when loss initially happened. Also know that you will likely not be the same person you were before the loss. Maybe tears will come more frequently. Maybe you will find yourself more empathetic to others going through pain. Maybe loss will teach you to truly appreciate what you have. You might find yourself slowing down more. Spending more time focused on the eternal or intentionally giving more time to building relationships with those who you truly care for. Do not be resistant to finding the positives that can come after loss. Do the positives outweigh the pain of the loss? Not really, but they can be a comfort as you will often find yourself growing or maturing in new areas.

Ecclesiastes 7:2 says, "It is better to go to the house of mourning than to go to the house of feasting, for this is the end of all mankind, and the living will lay it to heart." Why, give this rather morbid advice? Because, as uneasy as it can make one feel, the house of mourning will often point one to the eternal. The feasting and the pleasures of this life are temporary, but eternity will far outweigh any time spent on this blue ball. As a culture, western culture particularly, does not typically embrace this idea of coming close to death. We prefer to live in a fantasy that aging does not happen and even go so far as to deceive ourselves that death cannot touch us. The community college I attended put on a production of *Fame* that several of my friends were involved in. The musical ends with the cast singing about how they are going to live forever. I actually find this finale song a sad reminder of how much modern culture attempts to erase the uncomfortable reality of death—as if mortals could actually stop death.

Is this why so many people celebrate their 29th birthday at least ten times? So much money is spent every year on anti-aging products and hair dye to cover up the grey, but no product can ever completely delay the inevitable. Apart from the return of Christ, death will come at some point to each of us. Because of this reality, we should learn to live in such a way that this truth is reflected in our lives. It is a heavy reality. We love what we know. We wish we could control more than we can; but we cannot, and I think it is for this reason that the preacher in Ecclesiastes urges his readers to visit a house of mourning—the lessons it has to teach about how to live life can be sobering but also grounding.

That does not make it easy. Death and mourning are uncomfortable topics. No one wants to be around decay? Who is completely comfortable looking into the eyes of someone who is close to breathing their last breath? I know I am not. When we first came to PNG we fostered my husband's cousin's son Bradley for nine months. He is now back living with his father and grandmother who helped raise him after his mother passed away from cancer. We are spending Christmas in my husband's village this year, and when we arrived a week ago I heard that Bradley's grandma was near death. Her house is just down the road from ours. My husband immediately went to visit her, but I did not. I have meant to for the last few days, but then the sun goes down and another day goes by without me going. It is uncomfortable, so consciously or unconsciously I avoid it. I prefer situations where I can fix something, do something, bring hope or at least a helping hand. But, what can one offer in the face of death? This avoidance is common in a culture that has a tendency to confine death to solitary hospital rooms and spends millions of dollars dressing those who have passed away so they simply look like they are peacefully asleep. We push it away, pretending that death and decay cannot touch us or those we love. Avoid it at all costs. It is ugly—so people are often pressured to "move on" as quickly as possible and the tendency is to gloss over anything that might make one feel uneasy.

But, what if we are supposed to pause and sit in the uncomfortable? What if learning to live again is not so much about moving on but about stopping—stopping dead in our tracks so to speak? What if we are meant to sit with the pain, the uncomfortable,

> *But, what if we are supposed to pause and sit in the uncomfortable? What if learning to live again is not so much about moving on but about stopping—stopping dead in our tracks so to speak? What if we are meant to sit with the pain, the uncomfortable, and the reality of the fragility of life and let it change us?*

and the reality of the fragility of life and let it change us? Moving forward, learning to live, should not be about trying to get back to normal as quickly as possible. Instead, I believe, it should be about leaning in to allow the pain and healing process to change you into a more empathetic person. Having walked through the valley of death, and reached new pastures with matured eyes, many people are a better version of themselves with a softened heart full of lessons learned from time in the house of mourning.

I finally went to see Bradley's grandma today. With some homemade biscuits (or scones as they would say in PNG) I stopped putting it off and headed down the slippery, narrow path to her house. She was sitting just outside her grass-roofed hut on a low wooden bench, her walking stick lying by her feet. She had actually improved over the last week and was now able to eat some soft foods again. Her eldest son was there. We talked about family history and politics. One of her grandsons was playing marbles in the packed dirt by our feet. I asked her how many children she had and was told four boys and three girls, two of which have already passed away. She is mostly blind and very, very thin, but what a strong woman. It seemed that the morning visit did us both some good. She gave me a cabbage, and I headed back home. It all seemed strangely normal. I think the closer we allow ourselves to get to the process of no longer being on this earth the better we are for it. One day it will be us. What lessons will we have learned by that time? Learn to live—yes, but maybe we should also spend more time learning the lessons the dying have to teach.

> *"But may the God of all grace, who called us to His eternal glory by Christ Jesus, after you have suffered a while, perfect, establish, strengthen, and settle you."*
> *—1 Peter 5:10 (NKJV)*

A Child That Was Blessed

By Alison Holt

GRIEF IS A strange emotion that appears to have a memory all of its own. It can lie dormant for years and then bounce out when you least expect it. Time IS a great healer, but grief can operate in its own time zone. Ecclesiastes talks about "a time to be born and a time to die" (Ecclesiastes 3:2) and "a time to mourn and a time to dance" (Ecclesiastes 3:4). As Westerners we often interpret mourning as a one-off event– a person dies, I mourn, I move on. I have learnt so much from my Papua New Guinean friends, watching them mourn the death of loved ones and national leaders who have died as a direct or indirect result of COVID-19 raging through the land. My colleagues here are far closer to their roots of human-beingness in contrast to my human-doingness.

Mourning is a physical activity acknowledging a life well lived, and it can be a wonderful time to celebrate and commemorate. Yet we can feel guilty if we remember the dead with a laugh or a smile. Mourning and grieving can be somber activities, but just so as you know, I'm giving myself permission to mourn my Mother, not with the dirge like misery that my forebears would suggest would be appropriate, but with the fondness of a little girl remembering happy times with her Mum and knowing that I will see her again one day.

And this is where it starts to get tricky. My Mum died when I was seven years old, and she died at a time when counseling wasn't a thing, and in a country where the culture set the expectation that you would bury your dead at the earliest opportunity and get on with life. My family majored on "being stoic" and that resulted in us not talking about Mum for a good 20-30 years after she passed away. Even now, I have very few photos of Mum, but I remember her face, her voice and I remember the lovely sense of comfort and fun that she exuded. I remember cooking with her– making fish cake patties, I remember her friends coming round and sitting in deckchairs by the raspberry canes in the garden and their joyful laughing as they shared life together. I remember when the pressure cooker blew up, and I remember when Mrs. Miller fell straight through the aging canvas of one of the deck chairs. My Mum and the other ladies (including Mrs. Miller) laughed uncontrollably. Their laughter was infectious. I vaguely remember holidays away together as a family and big Christmases celebrated with family and friends and wonderful food and treats, but the lasting memories are from the everyday. I used to love "helping" Mum with the housework. As the local Brown Owl (Brownie Guide leader) Mum was very creative at encouraging voluntary participation. We had a wooden floor that she would add polish to before tying dusters to my feet and inviting me to try "ice skating." I learnt a lot from Mum about making the dreary things of life fun and about enjoying and appreciating the fun things of life. Mum introduced me to classical music, and I find it very exciting to go to live concerts to hear the performance of pieces that she played to me as a child. Mum also tried to introduce me to ballet, but I've never really got on top of left and right, and I was expelled at an early age. Mum had made me a lovely little white dress for ballet. It didn't get much use, but I do enjoy going to watch the ballet—her influence and enthusiasm has stuck with me.

The night Mum died I was out at Brownies. I remember kissing her goodbye as I left the house, and I remember her telling me that she was proud of me. It was a Friday evening. During our Brownie session the Vicar's wife arrived with an urgent message, and I was told to go to the Vicarage after Brownies had ended. I remember the Vicarage as a cold and heartless place, and the Vicar and his wife were as cold and frosty as their surroundings. The Vicar's wife fed me some cheese-on-toast and I remember noting at the time that it wasn't how my mum made cheese-on-toast. Eventually my father arrived in his grey overcoat. He had a heaviness and sadness about him that was palpable as he entered the room. I sat on his lap, and he told me the news—that Mum had died and that I was to stay the night at the Vicarage. I couldn't really take in what he said, and I don't think the news was real to him either. I spent a miserable night, cold and alone in a bed that smelt of damp and mothballs, surrounded by crucifixes and wondering why my family had abandoned me. Were they all dying? Was I going to be left all alone? Had Mum really died, or had she just gone to visit my Godmother in Australia? I consoled myself that Mum was ok, but she had gone away for a bit, and eventually I fell asleep.

And that was it. I went back home, and life carried on— almost as if nothing had happened. I was farmed out to friends for the funeral, and it was a long time before I really believed that Mum had actually died. School was ok—well, until we got to "making things for Mother's Day" or asking your mother to help or do something. I hadn't actually cried when my dad broke the news of Mum's death and for many years I was stuck with a tape running in my head that ran every time a tear-worthy event popped up, "You didn't cry when Mum died, so you can't cry now."

Three years later, my dear dad remarried. I think he was lonely and struggling to hold down a job that required him to commute to and from London every day and to raise three children on his own, despite the fact that my sister and brother were so much older than me. My first stepmother was a weird character and nasty with it—traditional fairy tale material! Within a year my brother and sister had left home for good. My friends were scared to come around to the house, and I spent as much time as possible away. I left home at the earliest opportunity, went to university, studied mathematics, found employment, got married and set up home at a different end of the country. We saw very little of Dad and my stepmother, and my new in-laws became like Mum and Dad to me. All was well.

Then one day, I was playing with my oldest two children who were aged three and one at the time. We were having a wonderful time together, and suddenly I was overwhelmed with tears and grief as it struck me (as if I'd been hit by a truck) that Mum should be here now to see my children. It still reduces me to tears when I think how much she would have loved the granny role and how much my children would have loved playing and hanging out with her. Friends prayed for me as I went through my time of grief. You can bury a person, but you can't bury grief. As the grief came out, memories emerged…and lots of questions. Why had I spent the night of my mum's death at the Vicarage? Why didn't I go to the funeral? Why couldn't I see Mum in hospital? My dad and I had long lost touch, but I felt the burning need to call him— not really knowing what the response would be. It was absolutely, totally, utterly wonderful. Dear Dad said that I was the first person to talk to him about Mum since she had died. He and I felt a surge of relief as we talked about her. As Dad answered my many questions, I realized that he had done his best at the time and that both he and Mum loved me very much.

From that point on, there were many times as my children were growing up that I recognized that my instinct to do or not do something, was my inheritance from Mum. She might have died when I was only seven, but she had planted many thoughts and ideas within me that would later flourish and bloom.

Dad and I still talk regularly about Mum and I feel I know her now as an adult person. The void of unknown and emptiness that was once filled with grief is being replenished with stories that bring love, joy, peace and grace.

I'm no longer a child that was abandoned by her Mother at an early and difficult age. I'm a child that was blessed to have had seven very precious years with her mum—years of being influenced by a dear and lovely woman of God, a woman who knew to plant ideas, thoughts and principles which would stick with me long after her death.

A Psalm for Reflection

Psalm 16

Keep me safe, O God,
for I have come to you for refuge.
I say to the LORD, "You are my Master!
Every good thing I have comes from you."
The godly people in the land
are my true heroes!
I take pleasure in them!
Troubles multiply for those who chase after other gods..
I will not take part in their sacrifices of blood
or even speak the names of their gods.

LORD, you alone are my inheritance, my cup of blessing.
You guard all that is mine.
The land you have given me is a pleasant land.
What a wonderful inheritance!

I will bless the LORD who guides me;
even at night my heart instructs me.
I will not be shaken, for he is right beside me.

No wonder my heart is glad, and I rejoice.
My body rests in safety.
For you will not leave my soul among the dead
or allow your holy one to rot in the grave.
You will show me the way of life,
granting me the joy of your presence
and the pleasure of living with you forever (NLT).

CHAPTER FOURTEEN

Sitting with Lament, Grieving with Hope

> "When we grieve over someone who has died in Christ, we are sorrowing not for them, but for ourselves. Our grief isn't a sign of weak faith, but of great love."
>
> —Billy Graham

There is a whole book in the Bible called Lamentations. A book dedicated to grief, expression of emotion, bitter weeping for a city that once was glorious but now lay in ruins. Betrayal, affliction, no rest, desolation, bitter anguish, weeping, suffering, anger, distress, torment, groaning, a faint heart, silence, dust, sackcloth, eyes that fail from weeping, a wound as deep as the sea, tears flowing like a river, no relief, darkness, a pierced heart, a downcast soul, terror, no prayer can get through, joy is gone from our heart... These are all words or phrases used in the book of Lamentations. It is honest and raw; not sugar coated in any way.

Tiny pockets of hope do appear like in chapter 3:22-26 "Because of the LORD's great love we are not consumed, for his compassions never fail. They are new every morning; great is your faithfulness, I say to myself, 'The LORD is my portion; therefore I will wait for him.' The LORD is good to those who hope in him, to the one who seeks him; it is good to wait quietly for the salvation of the LORD" (NIV). But this beautiful declaration of hope is very much in the minority. The majority of Lamentations is an uncensored look at the pain of loss. When reading it one cannot help but wonder why—if the creator of the universe saw the importance of including such an honest expression of emotion to loss in His love letter to mankind why do we, as the modern church, often avoid giving space for lament? Why do so many people try to dismiss or downplay the pain of loss? Let out your lament—the anguish, the weeping, the groaning, wrestle with the feeling that your prayers, at times, can feel like they are not getting through. God can handle those feelings, your doubt and anger. This is not how He created the world to be. Sin and death break His heart as they do ours. There was no ugliness of death in the beginning before sin entered paradise. Death was never the intention for the original creation. But, with the choice of free will, evil did enter a perfect paradise when the forbidden fruit was eaten.

    I think it is a mistake to downplay the pain that death can cause. There is nothing inherently good about it. It is the ugly result of sin, and sin and evil are the opposite of who God is. Yes, God can take even the worst pain and bring about good, but His good and perfect world was never meant to contain death. So lament, and encourage others to lament as well. Lament is a gift, in a way, because it allows someone time and space to express that—

what has happened hurts! And it is not how things were intended to be. Grieve and mourn that anyone has to be touched by something so ugly and life altering. Let us, especially as Christians, give space—just as the Bible does—for deep lament. In a sinless world your child would never have had to die. Your mother would have lived to see her grandchildren, if sin had not opened the door to disease. These pains should be lamented, and it should be the practiced norm to do so. What is not normal is not expressing how much death and disease can hurt. Pain points us, in a way, to God because even the non-Christian can see that the world is flawed, broken, not how it should be. Only a perfect heaven without the presence of sin and death can return things to the way they were intended. This is our comfort.

I do not think that these truths are new to most people and yet somehow there seems to be a disconnect of belief and practice. Why if we know that sin and death are so tragically opposed to God and his goodness, do we give so little space for lament? It is almost as if someone appears to be too affected by grief that they are not being a good Christian, not hoping enough in God, or even sinning in some way. The Bible, and even Jewish culture, do not reflect these ideas. I think that if we do not allow time to grieve something as painful as death then we cheapen the very real pain which, in Biblical times, often resulted in people physically tearing their clothes.

In Jewish culture, when someone dies there are practices that mourners are instructed to follow—these include reciting the Kaddish and sitting for Shiva. During the seven-day period (following the burial of a loved one) called Shiva, the family facing loss remains in their home and mourners come to be with them. During this period (which is observed after the loss of a parent, spouse, sibling or child) the Jewish law requires mourners to recite the Kaddish three times each day for seven day. For parents, the Kaddish (a prayer of praise to God) is then recited every day for eleven months following the burial. For other relatives it is recited during a thirty day mourning period which is called sheloshim.[36] These practices help ensure that those in mourning are given time and space to process grief.

So grieve. Grieve with hope knowing that God is a good God who has also experienced the deep pain that His children face. He is a high priest familiar with our sufferings. He gives space and time for His children to walk through dark valleys, but promises that the valley is not an endless one. He is at work right now preparing a place that will not be marred by death. This is our hope. This is why we grieve, but not like those who have no hope. Heaven—heaven is the hope that can keep our hearts and minds steady through even the most painful grief. So grieve, mourn and lament while still holding on to hope.

There are typically three parts to a Biblical lament and it has been estimated that around forty percent of the Psalms are written in this form of lament. These elements of lament are ***a cry to God, a request for help for God to move,*** and finally ***a response of trust and praise***. Lament can actually be a form of worship.[37] As we close the pages of this journey together I strongly encourage you to take time to write out your own lament. Writing a lament can be done in the form of poetry, prose or even as a song. Use whichever medium you feel the most comfortable with. Deep grief can also

> So grieve. Grieve with hope knowing that God is a good God who has also experienced the deep pain that His children face. He is a high priest familiar with our sufferings. He gives space and time for His children to walk through dark valleys, but promises that the valley is not an endless one.

be processed through art, something as simple as a stick drawing.

When taking the class on healing heart wounds participants were encouraged not only to write out a lament but also to process loss through drawing. At the time, I was still grieving a situation I had faced when I worked at a children's home in Kenya two years previous. I had the privilege of being part of a team that cared for nineteen children, but due to a lot of different factors, it became clear to the team that I was serving with that it was time for us to leave. This is probably one of the most painful decisions I have ever had to make. Within a day, we packed our things and left barely even having a chance to say good-bye to the children who had become such a huge part of our lives.

For years afterwards I would have vivid, painful recurring dreams where I was with the kids and then the lady who had started the home would suddenly show up and take them away. Since I was clearly still grieving this situation, I focused my lament on the grief I had faced in this situation, and I also wrote a letter expressing my grief and forgiveness towards the lady who had started the children's home. As part of the closing ceremony we had the opportunity to burn these letters. As I took out time to process, I drew a simple stick figure drawing to reflect emotions surrounding my grief—tears, an airplane, the kids and then on the other side of the paper a drawing of my son, who was just two-months old (at the time I took that class), a gift coming after so much pain of being separated from my Kenyan kids. I wrote out a lament as well and it felt good to get those intense feelings out on paper. Interestingly enough after taking the time to process (even several years after the fact) the reoccurring dreams stopped. I felt more peace, and it showed me again the value of taking time to sit with lament and process loss. Pain is still there, but healing has taken place as well, and I can see how God used that hard experience to guide my husband and me to serve in PNG, a place that has been such a blessing to our little family as we minister here.

As I wrap up this final chapter, it's Christmas Eve. I'm enjoying the mini Christmas miracle of having both of my busy kids napping at the same time! I can't even remember the last time that happened. We obviously do not get any snow in the village, but a calming rain has been falling most of the day. I'll take it. My mother-in-law just dropped by with a chunk of cooked pork that smells delicious and made me smile because I was just beating myself up mentally for not picking up some type of ham yesterday during our trek into town. I guess we will have a bit of pork for Christmas after all.

We spent yesterday attending the funeral for my husband's aunt, Keld, who passed away last Thursday. It took crossing two natural foot bridges and walking up part of a mountain to get to where the funeral was being held. As I sat on the grass and listened to what bits of language I could understand, I was reminded—yet again—the value of taking time to mourn with those who mourn. I was struck, in a strange sort of way, by the beauty of the many fresh flowers decorating the outdoor funeral area—almost like a wedding. I was amazed—yet again—how comforting music can be giving familiar, comforting words when one has no words due to heartbreak. For me, the eulogy was the most moving part of the service. Given by her husband, Fung, he simply told their story how his dad had told him to wait and marry this particular girl, one of the evangelist's daughters. Fung had joined the defense force (army) and even though other girls showed an interest in him, he faithfully stuck to what his dad had advised and married my husband's aunt. She was seventeen when they got married, seventy-nine when she passed away after struggling with an illness for the last five years. Love had united them until death, her husband had said; and they lived in peace, without fighting their entire lives together. "A piece of my body is now gone," he shared. "Darling, we will be united again in paradise." As I listened to such a sweet, heartfelt speech; I was touched. Everyone has a story, sadly it is often not until someone leaves this earth that you get to hear pieces of that story. As the casket, shrouded in a white and purple cloth, was carried out to be put in its final resting place all the family members—children, grandchildren (and I believe even some great-grandchildren) surrounded it. I thought, "What a legacy, generations that came into being because of this woman—a humble, village lady who spent her whole life in the mountains of Papua New Guinea living a quiet but full life."

Permission to Mourn

My husband's grandfather was an evangelist, one of the first people to help bring the gospel to some of the area villages where my husband is from. Now seeing one of his daughter's buried I saw how she had her own legacy in a way. It reminded me again how so many times in life people work so hard and spend their life chasing so many different things. However, it is often the simple, faithful life that is so extraordinarily beautiful—a life that will be rewarded, no doubt, in the next life to come. A few lessons gleaned from choosing to sit in a house of mourning.

So we mourn, and yet we hope. We cry, and yet those tears will one day be wiped away forever. May you, my friend, find comfort in your journey though it contains grief. May you find hope in the beauty that is to come—a perfect, new heaven and earth where death is conquered forever.

"He will swallow up death forever: and the Lord GOD will wipe away tears from all faces, and the reproach of his people he will take away from all the earth, for the Lord has spoken." —Isaiah 25:8

Lean Into the Pain

By Ruth Potinu

"IT'S JULY 16TH tomorrow, I said, or tried to say. I felt my throat tighten as I attempted to let my husband know that tomorrow was likely going to be a hard day. This year marks 25 years since my twin sister suddenly passed away from respiratory complications due to malaria, at least that is what the doctors think it might have been.

"I'll take the kids for a while," my husband thoughtfully responded. So while the house has been unusually quiet, I've flipped through a picture book looking back at memories of my twin sister who had just turned eight and a half the day she passed away. Spunky with a headful of golden, red curls Allison marched to her own beat, living her short life in a way that brought joy and laughter to many who crossed paths with her.

Last year, on the anniversary of my sister's death, I pushed my feelings back thinking that year would be a bit easier. My own little Allyson had been born earlier that year, which has been such a healing gift; but by the end of the day I was in tears. The more I acknowledge the hard days the more I find healing and peace in the memories. While my sister's grave is oceans away in the Democratic Republic of Congo, I can still take time out to remember her regardless of where my circumstances take me.

So I sat in the quiet, grateful for a bit of time to process and journal. Remembering helps my hurting heart grieve. I posted some thoughts on my virtual community of Instagram/Facebook. It was healing to read other people's responses. Some of those who commented knew Allison and were also deeply affected by her sudden death. Others never met her but wrote that they wished that they had been given the chance to. Some knew a bit of my story. Others had never heard it before. It did feel like mini virtual hugs to read the sweet comments people left. Sometimes community is close enough to give you a hug—sometimes it is miles away. I was able to briefly chat with my parents, and my mom said that she purposely wore a shirt that was made for her during her last trip to PNG because it felt like a hug from me.

In the past I have avoided bringing up the anniversary of my sister's death, but I am learning that I'm not the only one thinking about her on July 16th, and one way to mourn is to mourn both individually and collectively. After my husband came home with the kids we flipped through that photo album together. I answered my son Trevor's questions about aunty Allison and I gave my own little Allyson some extra snuggles. Healing happens. It is still hard even as the years pass, but there is a soothing balm in remembering. Each year is different. Some years are harder than others. Some years the tears come, other years they don't, but I'm learning to lean into the pain instead of avoiding it. I'm finding it important to create space (even small bubbles of space) to remember and celebrate a life that was and still is loved.

July 16th, 2010

Fifteen years ago today my twin sister Allison died. I wish I could go sit by her grave just to be there to tell her that I still miss her like crazy, but I can't because her grave is thousands of miles away in the Democratic Republic of Congo. Congo has been at war since 1996 and parts of it are still too dangerous to travel to, so I will have to content myself with writing.

Yesterday I was around a set of ten-year-old twins. One loves pink and had her finger nails painted, the other one loves everything camo. Watching them was almost like watching a dance as they discover the world together teasing each other at every turn. I enjoy being around twins, especially watching them interact, and yet it makes my heart ache because it reminds me what a precious relationship I have lost.

When Allison died, my friend Erika compared her death to a piece of candy wrapped in a candy wrapper. Allison left this world and went to heaven. In a sense, she got the candy Erika had explained. All of us left on earth just get the wrapper. Sure the wrapper can be sweet at times, but still it is just the wrapper—nothing compared to the actual candy. I never forgot that illustration, and yet it is hard at times knowing that I'm still here on earth while she is in heaven. We are twins which means we are supposed to be discovering life together teasing each other at every turn. It's hard that many of my best friends now never got the chance to even meet Allison. She was so witty, smart and beautiful—truly an angel in my eyes.

July 16th, 2020

Twenty-five years ago today my twin sister took her last breath at just eight years old. So I'm sitting here flipping through a picture book that my mom gave me as a Christmas present the year my own little Allyson was born. There are pictures of twin cuddles, two toddlers on the same bike, a meal shared with cousins the day Allison passed away. I see our last family photo when we flew out from our home in Africa. My brother has one of Allison's toys tucked in the strap of his waist bag. I am wearing a dress that my grandma sewed for my twin.

I also found myself clicking through pictures of the day my own daughter Allyson was born. I longed for a daughter and told my younger sister that she better not use the name Allison for any of her kids. But, a deep fear of mine was that I would never have a girl. Yet, she came, and I hold her every night and say her name probably 100 times a day. It does ease the pain.

I still miss you, Allison, your quirky personality, your strawberry blond curls. I miss the games we used to play and the imaginary adventures we would go on. You are forever my sister, my twin and my very best friend. It is not easy to think about you without tears creeping into my eyes. But, today I am thankful for photos, memories and for each day that I was able to spend with you.

A Psalm for Reflection

Psalm 23

The LORD is my shepherd;
I shall not want.
He makes me to lie down in green pastures;
He leads me beside the still waters.
He restores my soul;
He leads me in the paths of righteousness
For His name's sake.
Yea, though I walk through the valley of the shadow of death,
I will fear no evil;
For You are with me;
Your rod and Your staff, they comfort me.
You prepare a table before me in the presence of my enemies;
You anoint my head with oil;
My cup runs over.
Surely goodness and mercy shall follow me
All the days of my life;
And I will dwell in the house of the LORD
forever. (NKJV)

Hamö-kom y'na-chaym es-chem
b'soch sh' ör avay-lay
tzi-yon viru-shölö-yim

"May God comfort you among the other mourners of Zion and Jerusalem."

Meet the Contributors

TARA AMIS | Tara is a Speech-Language Pathologist turned stay-at-home homeschooling mama to three boys, Michael, Noah and Jeremiah. She and her husband Zack have a sweet daughter Isabella in heaven and plan to adopt in the near future. To add to the chaos, Tara sells books with Usborne Books and More with the mission of spreading literacy to as many kids as possible. The Amis family are also huge nerds and love playing games of all kinds with the desire of spreading the Gospel to the local gaming community.

KRISTEN BOE | Kristen is a displaced Jersey girl, who lives in St. Louis, Missouri with her husband, daughter and two cats. She serves as the director of a tutoring ministry that serves many immigrant and refugee children among others. Kristen is an avid reader, recreational writer and seasoned traveler.

STEPHANIE CLARKE | Stephanie is a pastor's wife and a thankful mom to two teenagers. She's originally from the Bluegrass State of Kentucky but lives and serves alongside her husband of 20 years in Barbados and the wider Caribbean region. She has a passion to write with the hope of encouraging others and also loves her morning walks, capturing all things creation on camera, the game of cricket, family vacations and a good cup of coffee. You can connect with Stephanie on her an Instagram @stephpclarke or on Facebook Stephanie Prater Clarke

DR. DONALD ERICKSON | After 33 years of serving as a senior pastor, Dr. Erickson and his wife, Claudia, are equipping pastors and church leaders internationally in a number of countries to include Honduras, Cuba, Zambia, Peru and Albania. He also serves as Area Superintendent in the Great Lakes District of the Evangelical Free Church of America shepherding more than twenty pastors. He and his wife have been married fifty years and have four children and two grandchildren.

ANN-MARIE FERRY | Ann-Marie is a writer from the Midwest. She is a wife of 10 years to Jon, the man she met online, and a mother to four children: three daughters on earth and a son in heaven. Ann-Marie's writing reflects on her experience with high-risk pregnancy and stillbirth through the lens of faith, shining the light of hope on grief. You can find her writing as a regular contributor for Sharing Magazine and on her website and annmarieferry.com.

HEATHER HOLDSWORTH | Heather is a Bible teacher, lecturer, writer, artist and lover of Earl Grey tea with friends. Her focus is in the subject of Spiritual Formation and Discipleship for people of all ages. Much of her art is a unique meditation on Scripture that may need a magnifying glass to appreciate. She lives in Scotland with Adrian, her husband of 24 years. You can connect with Heather on Instagram @hope.scapes and Facebook @hopescapes.home

ALISON HOLT | Since graduating as a mathematician in London in the 1980s, Alison has been blessed with an amazing and continually expanding family, and a career that has taken her around the world. She currently spends her time between Papua New Guinea and New Zealand. You can connect with her at Alison Holt LinkedIn.

DR. CRISTIAN S. ILE | Cris is a grateful child of God, Lindsey's happy husband, and the proud father of Zion, Eliana and David. He holds a PhD in theology and loves to teach the Bible.

BARB LAMB | Barb retired in May 2020 after teaching mathematics for 41 years at Cary-Grove High School. She still resides in Cary, IL and has two adult children, Elise and AJ. In retirement, she plans to continue to volunteer both at church and in the community and possibly do some traveling. She enjoys baking, gardening, working on various projects around the house and going to concerts with Elise and AJ. She can be reached at malamb25@gmail.com.

LEAH NELSON | Leah Nelson was saved by the grace of God at age 19. Since then, she has graduated Bible college, traveled the world for the sake of Christ and been involved in prison ministry and faith based rehabilitation ministries. Her passion is to help others find their ultimate joy in Christ. She is the wife of Philip and mother of Emet. Leah currently lives with her family in North Dakota where Philip serves as a youth pastor.

AMY POST | Amy lives in Indiana. She is a happy wife to a mechanical engineer and stay at home mom to two sassy little girls. She enjoys reading and baking and lives for a great cup of coffee.

AMANDA PRATHER | Amanda lives in Dublin, Ireland and hails from southern Illinois. She works in communications and fundraising for an international NGO. She enjoys traveling, reading, learning new things and photography. You can connect with Amanda on Instagram @aprather13.

SARAH PRICE | Sarah is a stay at home mom who lives in Illinois. She enjoys reading, crocheting and playing at the park with her daughter.

About the Author

Ruth Potinu is a missionary kid whose life was deeply affected by loss when her eight-year-old twin sister passed away suddenly while she and her family were living in the Democratic Republic of Congo. Due to that experience, Ruth has a heart to walk with others experiencing loss in their life. Having lived in several different cultures, Ruth has seen some amazing ways that those coming from more tribal focused mindsets often walk through grief together instead of avoiding it or leaving people to feel very alone during times of deep loss.

Acknowledgments

This book has been such a team effort which seems fitting for a book on learning to grieve in community. I could not have produced what is in your hands apart from so many people who have encouraged and inspired me along the way. Thank you, Amanda Prather, it was conversations with you, after your mom passed away and my dear friend Alice also died, that really birthed the idea for this book nine years ago. Thank you for your honesty, openness and willingness to engage with hard topics and also for being the first person willing to contribute your own grief story.

Thank you to Catherine Campbell. Eight years ago in a short conversation with you about this book you advised me to, "live a little more life first." I took that advice and this book is what it is today due, in part, to your words of wisdom.

Thank you to Maggie Comb, author of *Unsuper Mommy*, whose story helped inspire me that it is possible to write a book even when you have young kids. Thank you to Owen Makindi whose budgeting and goal setting workshop, two years ago, helped me prioritize again what was really on my heart to share and make needed steps to bring this book to life.

Thank you to Jamie Janosz for always being so generous with your time and advice and for reading some of the very first drafts of this book. You have such a gift of encouragement which has meant so much to me during this journey.

Michelle Warren, thank you. That conversation over pasta salad not long after I was recovering from dengue fever really helped me shape the book in my head more and start moving forward. To my Bible study ladies (here in PNG and those who have travelled to other countries) thank you for always being so supportive. I can't thank God enough for each of you.

Sarah Price, my amazing sister. Thank you for giving so much of your time to help with editing and also for contributing your story as well. I promise to bring you lots of tea and chocolate soon. Thank you to my mom, Marilyn Uehle. You used to tell me that since I'm dyslexic, I would need a good editor. Thank you for being willing to be one of those editors. Lydia Delgado, friend, thank you for also giving so much of your time editing and for your insightful comments. I know I can always count on you to keep it real. Thank you to Tracey Johnson for helping edit the book proposal. I'll bring you tea and chocolate as well.

Simon, where do I even start. Thank you for literally recovering this manuscript around the halfway point when my laptop crashed. Thank you for the times you took the kids so I could write. Thank you for also doing a final read through of the manuscript. You are a man of many, many talents; and I am blessed to get to do life by your side.

Jenny Erlingsson, once again words feel insufficient. Thank you for being my book doula! It feels appropriate that I got your email saying that you wanted to do this project together while in the midst of labor with my daughter. (Yes, I checked my email while in labor as I was in labor for over 24 hours and wanted distractions from the pain). Thank you for using your talents and experience to help birth this book. It has been such a pleasure getting to work with you. I can't recommend you enough.

Thank you Amy Post, Leah Nelson, Ann-Marie Ferry, Stephanie Clarke, Pastor Don Erickson, Tara Amis, Barb Lamb, Cris Ile, Kristen Flores, Heather Holdsworth, and Alison Holt for each sharing your honest grief story. Your powerful stories have literally changed me, and they are absolutely my favorite part of this book.

To Trevor, Allyson and Abigail. You each light up my little world so much. Thank you for being patient with me, as your mom, during this process and for all the inspiration you give me.

To my Savior, my Creator. Thank you for your living Word (especially the Psalms) and for never abandoning me in the valley of the shadow of death.

I wish there was space to mention each person's name who has walked with me through life's many painful moments. Thank you for sitting with me, crying with me, listening and loving me especially in those broken places. May beauty come from our collective pain.

Let's continue the conversation as we seek to provide spaces to grieve in community. Connect with us at

www.permissiontomourn.com

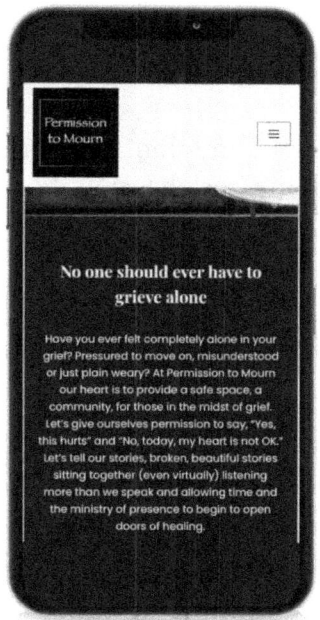

facebook.com/permissiontomourn

@permissiontomourn

Endnotes

1. Brody, Jane E. "The Biological role of Emotional Tears Emerges Through Recent Studies." *New York Times* (New York) 31 Aug. 1982, Section C, 1 www.nytimes.com/1982/08/31/science/biological-role-of-emotional-tears-emerges-through-recent-studies.html.
2. In most English translations of the Bible John 11:35 is the shortest verse in the Bible with only nine characters, but in the original Greek this verse has 16 characters making it come in third place after 1 Thessalonians 5:16 (14 characters) and Luke 20:30 which in Greek has only 12 characters. patrickoben.com/shortest-verse-in-the-bible/
3. Devine, Megan. *It's OK That You're Not OK: Meeting Grief and Loss in a Culture That Doesn't Understand.* Sounds True, 2017. page 12, Permission granted by Sounds True and author Megan Devine
4. Ibid page 62,
5. Hill, Margaret, Harriet Hill, Richard Bagge, and Pat Miersma *Healing Wounds of Trauma: How the Church can Help.* Summer Institute of Linguistics, 2006 page 25 Chart used with permission
6. "Aberfan" *The Crown.* writing by Peter Morgan, directed by Benjamin Caron, season 3, episode 3, Left Bank Pictures and Sony Pictures Television, 2019.
7. Ibid
8. Gregory, Christina (Sept 23, 2020) PhD PSYCOM "The Five Stages of Grief: An Examination of the Kubler-Ross Model" *psycom.net* www.psycom.net/depression.central.grief.html

9. Moon, Erin Hicks *Lent Primer.* self-published, 2020. pages 9-10. Permission given.
10. Boehm, Nathan. "How Many Times Does the Bible Say Fear Not?" *Word Nuggets: Overlooked Treasures,* 2 March, 2009, wordnuggets.wordpress.com/2009/03/02/how-many-times-does-the-bible-say-fear-not/
11. Pryor, Matthew. "The Most Frequent Command in the Bible" *crosswalk.com,* 16 May, 2016, www.crosswalk.com/faith/bible-study/the-most-frequent-command-in-the-bible.
12. Devine, Megan *It's OK That You're Not OK: Meeting Grief and Loss in a Culture That Doesn't Understand* (Boulder: Sounds True, 2017) 12, 48. Permission granted by Sounds True and author Megan Devine
13. Weaver, Johanna. *Having a Mary Heart in a Martha World: Finding Intimacy with God in the Busyness of Life.* Waterbrook Press, 2000, 2002. pages 39-40. Permission Given Penguin Random House
14. Fitzpatrick, Elyse and Eric Shumacher, hosts "Interview with Vaneetha Rendall." episode 51, *Worthy: Celebrating the Value of Women* 18 Jan 18, 2021, Content quoted from the Worthy Podcast- Permission given by Elyse Fitzpatrick and Eric Shumacher worthycelebratingthevalueofwomen.libsyn.com/episode-51-interview-with-vaneetha-randall
15. To hear Patrick's testimony of recovering from covid check out his story here: www.youtube.com/watch?v=O9w_vzSGPq8
16. Kushner, Harold S. *When Bad Things Happen to Good People.* First Anchor Books Edition, 2004, 1981. page 47.
17. Beless, Hunter, host. "Goodness with Joni Eareckson Tada." *JourneyWomen Podcast,* 25 November, 2019. www.journeywomenpodcast.com/episode/goodness
18. *The Problem of Pain* by CS Lewis copyright CS Lewis Pte Ltd 1940. Extract used with permission.
19. Daveport, Chris, Benjamin Hastings and Ben Tan "Season" *Christmas: The Peace Project* Hillsong Worship, 2017.

20. Ziegler, Scott The Bridge Church Des Plaines, IL Dec. 7, 2008. Quote used with permission
21. Anderson, Hannah *All That's Good: Recovering the Lost Art of Discernment.* Moody Publishers, 2018. pages 69. Permission given.
22. Behind the Name. 29 May 2020, www.behindthename.com/name/solomon
23. Fitzpatrick, Elyse and Eric Shumacher, hosts "Interview with Maggie Combs." episode 50, *Worthy: Celebrating the Value of Women* 11 Jan. 2021. Permission given by both Elyse Fitzpatrick and Eric Shumacher worthycelebratingthevalueofwomen.libsyn.com/episode-50-interview-with-maggie-combs
24. For the full story you can visit www.simplycontemplating.wordpress.com/2016/10/27/the-story-i-couldnt-write-part-i/ and www.simplycontemplating.wordpress.com/2016/11/01/the-story-i-couldnt-write-part-ii/
25. Hart, Joseph (1721-1768). "How Good is the Lord We Adore"
26. "Hoops for Life 5K honors Sahara 'Hoops; Aldridge" KFVS12, 20 July 2011 *www.kfvs12.com/story/15113059/hoops-for-life-honors-sahara-hoops-aldridge/*
27. McDonald, Mary Ashby. *The Magnet: A Large-Animal Veterinarian's Journey.* XulonPress Elite, 2017 Location 2782 of 4474. Permission given by Author
28. For a helpful podcast on rejoicing with those who rejoice and mourning with those who mourn check out the episode "Joy and Sorrow with Abby Wedgeworth" on the JourneyWomen Poscast www.journeywomenpodcast.com/episode/joyandsorrow?rq=weep
29. Weaver, Johanna. *Having a Mary Heart in a Martha World: Finding Intimacy with God in the Busyness of Life.* Waterbrook Press, 2000, 2002. page 199. Permission Given by Penguin Random House

Endnotes

30. Montgomery, Lucy Maud. *Anne's Hours of Dreams.* Bantam Books, 1922, 1981, 1987. page 127. Fair Use.
31. Kushner, Harold S. *When Bad Things Happen to Good People.* First Anchor Books Edition. 2004, 1981. page 146. Permission given from Penguin Random House
32. Guthrie, Nancy. *What Grieving People Wish You Knew: About What Really Helps (and What Really Hurts).* Crossway, 2016. page 36 Used by permission of Crossway, a publishing ministry of Good News Publishing, Wheaton, IL 60187 www.crossway.org.
33. Ibid pages 50 and 56
34. Risner, Vaneetha Rendall (October 21, 2016) "How to Discourage a Suffering Friend" (October 21, 2016) *crosswalk.com* www.crosswalk.com/faith/spiritual-life/how-to-discourage-a-suffering-friend.html. Permission given by Author
35. For a fascinating look into Mary's ongoing journey with Cystic Fibrosis check out the Frey Life's daily vlogs on youtube at https:www.youtube.com/channel/UCFJY0O-pkdXs6YuM5KW7r7g
36. Mount Sinai Memorial Chapels."The Minyan and the Kaddish Reciting." *Mourning Customs*, 4 March 2021, www.msmc.us/the-minyan-the-kaddish/
37. Fox, Christina, "The Way of Lament." *Ligonier Ministries*, 6 May 2016 www.ligonier.org/blog/way-lament

www.ingramcontent.com/pod-product-compliance
Lightning Source LLC
Chambersburg PA
CBHW071959110526
44592CB00012B/1145